C000023267

EPIC eXplorers

Five fun and flexible sessions

Exploring the life of Jesus with children aged 4-11

Epic Explorers – Leader's Guide
Copyright © 2014 Christianity Explored / The Good Book Company
www.ceministries.org

Published by The Good Book Company Ltd
Tel (UK): 0333 123 0880
Tel (International): +44 (0) 208 942 0880
Email: info@thegoodbook.co.uk

Websites:
UK: www.thegoodbook.co.uk
North America: www.thegoodbook.com
Australia: www.thegoodbook.com.au
New Zealand: www.thegoodbook.co.nz

Design by André Parker and ninefootone creative.
Illustration by André Parker.
ISBN: 9781909919693 Printed in the Czech Republic

Welcome to Epic Explorers

Telling children the good news about Jesus is an exciting prospect, an act of obedience, and a big responsibility.

- It's an **exciting prospect** because the good news is so good, and children often respond to it more enthusiastically than adults!

- It's an **act of obedience** because, throughout the Bible, we see time and again commands to teach and train children, and to pass on God's mighty acts to the next generation. The Great Commission (Matthew 28:19-20) does not have an "adult only" rating!

- It's a **big responsibility** because, while we want to seize the brilliant opportunities we have, we don't want to over-simplify the gospel message or coerce impressionable children into a choice they haven't thought through. Rather, we ought to be careful, faithful and God-dependent, praying that God will unveil their eyes, and cause them to love him with all their heart and delight in him for ever.

Epic Explorers is ideal for a children's holiday club or vacation Bible school. The flexible sessions can also be used in a weekly evangelistic group, a short series in a regular club, or a children's *Christianity Explored* course.

The material helps you, and those in your care, journey through Mark's Gospel over five fun and interactive sessions (with an optional family session). Using the setting of Adventure Island, you will explore significant events from Jesus' life to discover **who Jesus is**, **why he came** and **what it means to follow him**.

Epic Explorers is full of creative ideas for reaching and teaching 4-11s, and flexible material that allows you to adapt it for your own context. We hope it will be useful for both the experienced children's worker and the first-time leader, whether you are reaching those with little or no church background, or teaching those who are already part of the church family.

May God richly bless you in all you do for the honour and glory of Christ.

Nate Morgan Locke, Tamar Pollard
and the Christianity Explored Team, November 2014

3

Section 1: How to use Epic Explorers   7

Section 2: Leader's guide   43

Appendices   147

How to use Epic Explorers

Teaching programme

Epic Explorers is based on Mark's Gospel. The children will first consider **who Jesus is** (his *identity*) as they hear how he called his disciples, performed miracles, showed his authority and revealed himself to be the Son of God (Mark 1).

They will then learn about **why Jesus came** (his *mission*) as they explore the problem of sin and the offer of forgiveness (Mark 2).

Having heard the truth about the reality of judgment, his substitutionary death, and his resurrection (Mark 15 and 16), the final session, looking at Mark 8, will help the children understand **what it means to follow Jesus** (his *call*).

Session	Main aim	Teaching passage
1. Breathtaking Bay	Children will... • Know that Jesus has authority over everything. • Understand that Jesus is God's Son.	Mark 1:1, 16-34
2. Discovery Dens	Children will... • Know that we don't treat God as we should, and that our biggest problem is our sin. • Understand that only Jesus has power to forgive sin and can rescue us.	Mark 2:1-17
3. Mysterious Mountains	Children will... • Know that Jesus' death was planned. He took the punishment we deserve for our sin. • Understand that, through Jesus' death, there's now a way for us to be forgiven friends with God.	Mark 15
4. Crown Cave	Children will... • Know that Jesus really did die and rise again. • Understand that, because Jesus has beaten death, we can know life in him.	Mark 16:1-8
5. Rocky Road	Children will... • Know that Jesus is God's Son and came to rescue us. • Understand that following Jesus means putting him first, even when it's tough.	Mark 8:27-35
Family event (at the end of the club/ course)	Parents will... • Be introduced to who Jesus is, understand why he came on a rescue mission, and discover what it means to follow him. • Be encouraged to attend a *Christianity Explored* course for themselves.	Summary of all five passages

Epic Explorers works best as a five-day holiday club or vacation Bible school. However, if you are running it over four days (or weekly for four weeks), sessions 3 and 4 could be combined.

At the end of both of the session 3 talks, you will find optional paragraphs that will help you to briefly cover the core teaching on the resurrection.

In the small groups, you will need to select two or three questions from each day of the activity booklet so that the groups think about both Jesus' death and his resurrection.

THE CORE COMPONENTS

There are three core components that should be included in your teaching, regardless of the context. These are:

1. An introductory group activity

2. A Bible talk

3. Group discussion

These may vary slightly in length, depending on your setting and the age of the children. Below are some suggested timings for each component, and how they may fit within different programmes.

Option A: Two-and-a-half-hour holiday club or vacation Bible school

An hour with everyone together including:

5 min	**Introductory activity**
10 min	**Bible talk**
5 min	Memory verse
5 min	Prayer
10 min	Quiz
	Challenges
	Songs

An hour to 75 minutes rotating round three activities (20 minutes in each):

20 min	Craft
20 min	Games
20 min	**Discussion groups** and refreshments

Up to 30 minutes all together at the end. Activities could include:

2nd part of the quiz

Serial drama

More songs

A game for families to join in (invite them to come 15 minutes early each day). Alternatively you could serve refreshments for them in another part of the building and have some team members chatting with them.

Option B: One-hour themed session, eg: on a Sunday

10 min	**Introductory activity**
10 min	**Bible talk**
10 min	**Discussion groups**
10 min	Game
10 min	Themed craft
5 min	Memory verse
5 min	Prayer time

Option C: 40-minute session, eg: 8-11s in a "course" setting

10 min	**Introductory activity**
10 min	**Bible talk**
20 min	**Discussion groups** with snacks

Option D: 25-minute session, eg: part of a midweek club

5 min	**Introductory activity**
10 min	**Bible talk**
10 min	**Discussion groups**

INTRODUCTORY ACTIVITY (CORE COMPONENT)

This is a short fun activity with the intention of introducing the theme of the session, as well as providing opportunities for the children to get to know one another and build relationships with the leaders.

For each session there are several options to choose from, always including one based on the children's activity books: *Epic Scratch Pad* (4-7s) and *Epic Logbook* (8-11s).

Before the session, choose the activity that will work best in your setting, make sure you have all the necessary equipment, and think through your explanation of the game.

BIBLE TALK (CORE COMPONENT)

For each session there are two suggested talks, one for a wider age-range of 4-11 year-olds, and one for older children (8-11s).

The talks make the "big idea" clear and memorable, and have applications that are closely connected, age-appropriate and specific. They are faithful to the passage, and are visual and accessible, aiming to help the children to engage with the Bible passage.

What the leader actually says to the children is shown in **bold type**. Directions to the leaders are in normal type.

DISCUSSION GROUPS (CORE COMPONENT)

This is a chance to consider further the Bible passage and its implications with the children in your group, using the activity books: *Epic Scratch Pad* (4-7s) and *Epic Logbook* (8-11s).

These times provide the opportunity to consolidate, as well as allowing children the chance to ask questions and build relationships with the team members. It is therefore important that those running the groups are well trained and well prepared. You will find training notes on pages 35-41.

The discussion-group material is differentiated for different age groups (4-7s and 8-11s). The activities and discussion questions differ in the *Epic Scratch Pad* and *Epic Logbook*, though they both build on the same core teaching from each session.

ADDITIONAL MATERIAL

Other teaching material within the book includes ideas for teaching the memory verse for the sessions (Mark 10:45) and for praying with the children.

There is a diverse range of activities in *Epic Explorers*, allowing to you to pick and mix challenges, quizzes, games, crafts, refreshments and songs, to go alongside your core components.

Some activities are there simply to help children get to know you and let off steam. These are tied in to the exploration theme. Others are intentionally designed to consolidate the main teaching point ("big idea") of the session.

FAMILY EVENTS

Epic Explorers is designed to help churches reach whole families, not just children, within the local community.

There are three suggested activities that you could run to help engage with non-Christian parents, build relationships and connect them into an adult *Christianity Explored* course.

There are ideas for:

- A family treasure hunt (including a wet-weather option)
- A family fun night
- A family service

Choose at least one to run at the end of *Epic Explorers*. Two summary talks, as well as programme outlines, have been provided on page 135.

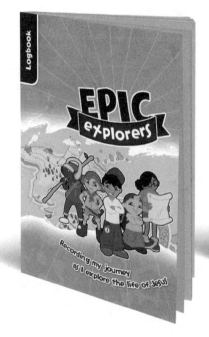

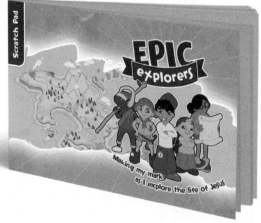

Unpacking the programme options

The material is flexible and can be adapted to fit into a reduced or extended amount of time. A five-day holiday club or vacation Bible school is ideal and will allow plenty of time to explore each day's theme. You can give extra time and resources to preparing a special event for local children and their families to enjoy.

A weekly club means you will have less time together, a smaller team and less of an explorer's theme (eg: decorating the venue would be difficult). However it may allow some leaders to be involved who can't do daytimes, and it will help build on-going relationships both with children and their families as you see them over a period of time.

On the following pages there are some details of suggested formats (also available as downloads from www.ceministries.org/epic).

As you consider which format to opt for, make sure you work out how much you can realistically fit in within your time slot. Ensure that enough time is given to teach the Bible passage clearly and unpack it further in discussion groups.

Option A: Two-and-a-half-hour holiday club or vacation Bible school – page 14

Option B: One-hour themed session, eg: on a Sunday – page 17

Option C: 40-minute session, eg: 8-11s in a "course" setting – page 18

Option D: 25-minute session, eg: as part of a midweek club – page 19

OPTION A: TWO-AND-A-HALF-HOUR HOLIDAY CLUB OR VACATION BIBLE SCHOOL

Time	Activity		Leader
	Tick when materials are ready for each activity	✔	
Before event	Those running the discussion groups to prepare their material.		
One hour before	Team meeting for Bible thought (download from www.ceministries.org/epic), prayer and final instructions.		
15 minutes (doors open 5 minutes before the session)	Register children as they arrive. **Map it out!** A brief game to introduce the theme (see introductory activities, page 60*). This can be done EITHER from the front stage with all the children together, OR within the discussion groups they'll be in later. *Page nos. are for Session 1. All sessions have activities listed in the same order.*		
50 minutes altogether	**Expedition time** • Theme song • Challenge (see Ideas Menu, page 64*) • Song • Memory verse (see Ideas Menu, page 62*) • Prayer (see Ideas Menu, page 63*) • Challenge (see Ideas Menu, page 64*) • Song • Bible talk (see pages 56-59*) • Quiz (see page 53*) • Theme Song		
60-75 minutes (Allow time for moving children from one area to another)	**Round and round.** Split the children into age-groups and rotate them around the three activities – 20 minutes on each: • Action adventures – games (see Ideas Menu, page 49) • Intrepid inventions – crafts (see Ideas Menu, pages 47 & 63*) • Discovery discussions – discussion groups (see Ideas Menu, pages 65-68*). Serve refreshments in this slot.		
15 – 30 minutes	**Explore all the more** • Song • Drama • 2nd part of the quiz or a family game** (adapt one of the challenges, page 64*) • Theme Song		
Afterwards	Team time for debrief, prayer and preparation for next session.		

** If you're not doing a family game, then consider serving refreshments for parents in another part of the building and have team chatting with them.

Each day's programme for a holiday club or vacation Bible school contains the following elements:

BIBLE PASSAGE

All the sessions are Bible-centred.

AIM

The aim is the "big idea" taught during the session. It is Bible-based.

PRE-SESSION TEAM MEETING

Notes to help you prepare your team for the session, including:

- A brief devotion on the Bible passage being taught (team devotions are available to download from www.ceministries.org/epic)
- Ideas for things to pray about
- Final comments on the day's arrangements

MAP IT OUT (10-15 MINUTES)

Register the children as they arrive at *Epic Explorers*. Then, depending on your premises, they will either go to the main venue where an introductory activity or two will be led from the stage, or into their "discovery discussion" groups.

If the children are all together, the introductory activity will help set up the day's focal point in an energetic and fun atmosphere.

If the children are in their groups, this time can be used for a short game and checking who can remember the memory verse. Younger children may find this option easier.

This short ten-minute section allows for late arrivers to join before the main teaching, as well as allowing you to introduce the day's theme.

EXPEDITION TIME (50 MINUTES)

This section of the programme should be pacy, fun-filled and action-packed. It will be led from the front with all the children together and contains the main Bible teaching as well as the other elements as explained below.

The Ideas Menu on pages 60-64* gives details.

Singing – is an enjoyable way to fix good words and biblical truths in the children's minds quickly. Therefore, look at the lyrics carefully and make sure you include some non-confessional songs so that children are not singing words they don't mean. Encourage your team to join in any actions – the children will only be as enthusiastic as the team are!

See page 150 for the *Epic Explorers* theme song.

Challenges – can be used to create team spirit and an enthusiastic environment. If you have divided the children into teams, it's good to involve a child from each one.

Memory verse – Mark 10:45 is the memory verse for the week.

> "*For even the Son of Man did not come to be served, but to serve, and to give his life as a ransom for many.*"

Since the verse will help the children understand who Jesus is and why he came, the person teaching it needs to include clear and concise explanation, repetition, actions or visual cues. There are creative suggestions for how the verse can be taught on page 62*.

Prayer – see page 63* for some creative prayer ideas that everyone can join in with.

Talk – this is when the Bible passage is taught. It is one of the core components, so should be prepared well and delivered clearly (see pages 56-59*).

Quiz – this should be seen as fun and enjoyable, but also a key part of the overall teaching, so...

- Ask questions that reinforce main points of the story, as well as some on the verse and songs.
- There needs to be variety in the way the questions are asked: *Factual* – who, what, why, when, where, how; *Multiple choice* – make all possibilities plausible; *Matching pairs* – ask a child to give the missing one; *True or false*; *Complete the verse* or fill in the missing word.
- A range of children need to be asked and their answers repeated so all can hear.
- Be fair – make sure that each team's questions are of the same level of difficulty.
- Explain the rules and stick to them (how many chances, hand over to other team, etc).
- Be exciting – encourage quick answers and cheering.

*Page numbers are for Session 1. All the sessions have activities listed in the same order.

ROUND AND ROUND (60-75 MINUTES)

Rotating around activities means there is more space for games and craft, and a quieter area for discussions. The three elements are Action adventure, Intrepid inventions and Discovery discussions.

ACTION ADVENTURES (20 MINUTES)

Games give children the chance to stretch their legs and burn off their energy. They are also a good way for children to build friendships with their peers.

It is good to prepare the games in advance and to tie them in to the exploration theme. A different type of games session each day will add variety. See page 49 for ideas.

INTREPID INVENTIONS (20 MINUTES)

Craft time is a great opportunity to chat to the children and follow up the things they have been learning. There are suggestions on page 63* for Bible-themed crafts, as well as exploration-themed ones (page 47). There are also ideas for thematic snacks, which could be made and then eaten in the Discovery Discussions.

DISCOVERY DISCUSSIONS WITH REFRESHMENTS (20 MINUTES)

These times are designed to reinforce the children's learning and give them opportunity to ask questions. See page 37 for further explanation of this core component.

It's good to use a small part of your discussion groups to plug the family specials and regular clubs.

EXPLORE ALL THE MORE (15-30 MINUTES)

During this time, all the children are back together and led from the front. Parents could be invited to come along to this slot, which includes some of the elements above, as well as the…

EPIC EXPLORERS DRAMA

Follow the adventures of five epic explorers as they travel around Adventure Island.

OPTION B: ONE-HOUR THEMED SESSION, EG: ON A SUNDAY

Time	Activity	Leader	
	Tick when materials are ready for each activity	✔	
Before event	Those running the discussion groups to have prepared their material.		
30 minutes before	Team meeting for Bible thought (download from www.ceministries.org/epic), prayer and final instructions.		
10 minutes	Register children and a brief game to introduce the theme (see Introductory activities, page 60*). *Page nos. are for Session 1. All sessions have activities listed in the same order.*		
10 minutes	Bible talk (depending on the age range of the group, it may be more appropriate to use the talks pitched at a wider age range, see pages 56-59*).		
10 minutes	Discussion groups – keep the children in the same groups each week.		
10 minutes	Game to consolidate the teaching (select from the introductory activities and tweak the explanation).		
10 minutes	Themed craft, related to the Bible story (see the Ideas menu, page 63*).		
5 minutes	Memory verse (see Ideas Menu, page 62*).		
5 minutes	Prayer (see Ideas Menu, page 63*).		
Afterwards	Team time for debrief, prayer and preparation for next session.		

OPTION C: 40-MINUTE SESSION, EG: 8-11s IN A "COURSE" SETTING

Time	Activity		Leader
	Tick when materials are ready for each activity	✔	
Before event	Those running the discussion groups to have prepared their material.		
30 minutes before	Team meeting for Bible thought (download from www.ceministries.org/epic), prayer and final instructions.		
10 minutes	Register children and a brief game to introduce the theme (see Introductory activities, page 60* – the activity in the Scratch Pad or Logbook would work well in this context). *Page nos. are for Session 1. All sessions have activities listed in the same order.*		
10-15 minutes	Bible talk (see pages 56-59*).		
15-20 minutes	Discussion groups (see pages 65-68*) – keep the children in the same groups each week. Have snacks while chatting.		
Afterwards	Team time for debrief, prayer and preparation for next session.		

OPTION D: 25-MINUTE SESSION, EG: AS PART OF A MID-WEEK CLUB

Time	Activity		Leader
	Tick when materials are ready for each activity	✔	
Before event	Those running the discussion groups to have prepared their material.		
One hour before	Team meeting for Bible thought (download from www.ceministries.org/epic), prayer and final instructions. Set up club.		
30 minutes (optional)	Club activities (eg: if your usual club lasts for an hour, start with these). Children arrive, register and join in the regular programmed activities.		
5 minutes	Brief game to introduce the theme (see Introductory activities, page 60*). *Page nos. are for Session 1. All sessions have activities listed in the same order.*		
10 minutes	Bible talk – depending on the age range of the club, it may be more appropriate to use the talks pitched at a wider age range.		
10 minutes	Discussion groups (see pages 65-68*) – keep the children in the same groups each week.		
5-10 minutes	Notices and a short game to end.		
Afterwards	Team time for debrief, prayer and preparation for next session.		

Aims

Epic Explorers will provide enjoyable, imaginative and controllable ways of sharing the good news of Jesus with children and families in your area. All formats aim to teach the identity, mission and call of Jesus. In addition, each session will have specific aims stated at the start of each section.

Alongside these aims, you will need to decide what your particular objectives are for *Epic Explorers*. This will help you choose which format to use. For example:

■ **An *Epic Explorer* holiday club or vacation Bible school** might be ideal for reaching those who:
- Have never really heard the gospel.
- Are loosely connected in some way to the church.

■ **An *Epic Explorer* course** might be ideal for those who:
- Are wanting to reach out to their friends and could bring them along.
- Have made a commitment and are looking to be grounded in the basics of what they believe.

■ **An *Epic Explorer* teaching programme in your weekly children's work** might be ideal for those who:
- Come along regularly but are not yet Christians.
- Have already attended holiday clubs and you hope to renew contact with to help their understanding further develop.

The course material is written to include ideas for a variety of settings and groups, but you must adapt it to suit your particular aims, group and circumstances.

It may be helpful to work through the concentric circles on the next page to establish which your primary aims are and how you will be able to evaluate the event afterwards to see if they were met. The purpose of the circles is to show the different stages we go through in our evangelism and discipleship. It is useful to consider which main stage your event is targeted at and the next stage you are aiming for.

Once you have set your aims, you will be able to make decisions on how many children you are hoping will attend, what age range you are looking at and how long you will run *Epic Explorers* for (eg: will you combine sessions 3 and 4?).

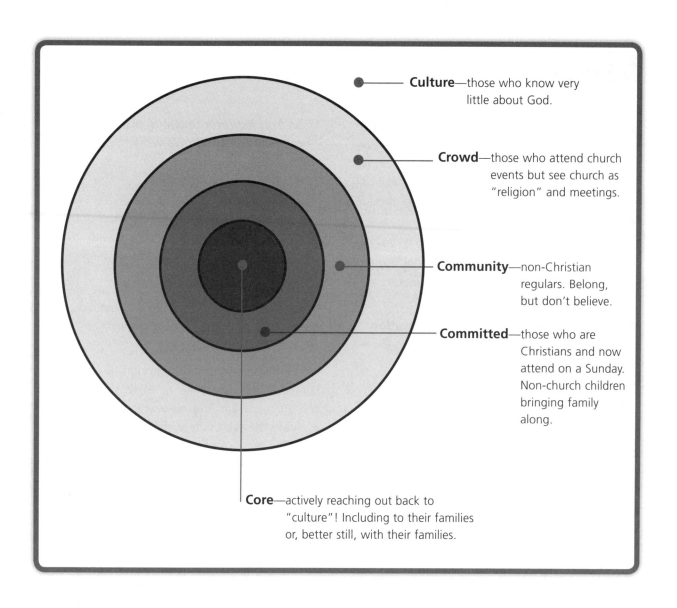

Culture—those who know very little about God.

Crowd—those who attend church events but see church as "religion" and meetings.

Community—non-Christian regulars. Belong, but don't believe.

Committed—those who are Christians and now attend on a Sunday. Non-church children bringing family along.

Core—actively reaching out back to "culture"! Including to their families or, better still, with their families.

Timetable for putting on Epic Explorers

FOUR MONTHS OR MORE BEFORE THE EVENT

- Decide what your primary aims are for *Epic Explorers;* and then which format you will be using, including which family event you will do.

- Decide what ages you are going to offer the event to and whether you will split it down into smaller age groups.

- Set the dates and check they don't clash with anything important (either within the church or local schools).

- Talk to your church leadership about your aims and how they fit in with the church's vision and programme, eg: will there be an adult *Christianity Explored* course soon after, that you can encourage parents to attend. Check that the church leadership is in support of *Epic Explorers*.

- Budget for *Epic Explorers*. Consider costs including *Epic Logbooks* and *Scratch Pads*, Mark's Gospels, refreshments, craft material, material for scenery, and prizes.

THREE MONTHS OR MORE BEFORE THE EVENT

- Publicise the dates to the congregation and think about how many team members you need to recruit.

- If you are running a holiday club or vacation Bible school, consider long-term craft and decoration preparation (eg: what resources do you need the congregation to be saving?).

- Decide how you are going to promote the event in schools, in clubs and at church.

- Work out your programme priorities, as you may not have time to fit everything in. Look at how best to include the vital core components.

TWO MONTHS OR MORE BEFORE THE EVENT

- Hold an open meeting of interested individuals for brainstorming ideas. Within the meeting, look at some of the key elements of Mark's Gospel using the *Identity, Mission and Call* framework (see page 35).

- Estimate attendance.

- Order any needed materials.

- Compile registration list.

- Send publicity to print.

- If you are running a holiday club or vacation Bible school, start making the decorations and choose songs for the week. Adapt the drama if needs be, now that you know who's on your team.

ONE MONTH OR MORE BEFORE THE EVENT

- Plan the details. If you are running a holiday club or vacation Bible school, include allocated time for drama and music practices, use of activity areas, etc.

- Distribute registration forms and publicity.

- Delegate teaching and organisational roles.

- Have two further team meetings with some training incorporated. Training is outlined on pages 35-41.

ONE WEEK BEFORE THE EVENT

- Complete decorations.

- Check supplies.

DURING EPIC EXPLORERS

- Arrive early for each session – take time for devotions, prayer and preparation.

- Watch for areas that may need adjustment.

- After the children leave, have a brief team meeting to evaluate, pray and look ahead.

THE WEEK AFTER EPIC EXPLORERS

- "Thank you's" to the team.

- Collect evaluations and suggestions from team.

- Photo display for congregation (let them know what they missed).

- Write to any un-churched families, reminding them about other upcoming events or regular church-based clubs.

Publicity

Once you have decided on the dates and timings of *Epic Explorers*, and have started the team recruitment process, the next big thing to work on is making sure children come! Packs of invitation cards are available that you can print with your own details (www.ceministries.org/epic).

There are also downloadable fliers and logos on the website, but if you are designing your own invitation then make sure it is visually attractive and the following things are clear:

• Who is running the event.

• When, where and at what time the event is on.

• For which ages the event is for.

• What kinds of activities are on offer.

• Whether there is a cost.

• Who to contact for further information.

Who you are aiming at will determine the amount of publicity you produce as well as your distribution of publicity. Whether you are running *Epic Explorers* as part of your midweek clubs, a special holiday club or vacation Bible school, or as a course, advertise it in your church bulletin and notices and within your regular children's groups. Why not send an invitation to every child you church has contact with?

If you are running it as a course, you might first want to do a study or two on the importance of evangelism with your existing churched chil-

dren and encourage them to pray about inviting friends along.

Posters in public places are another way of advertising the events, as are invitations in schools. Schools are often willing to give out fliers – and even more likely to do so if you put the fliers into class sets of thirty five! It is also useful to pass them on to the schools in advance so they have plenty of time to distribute them to the children.

Some schools may be happy for you to run a promotional assembly (or act of collective worship), especially those schools where your church already has contacts. If you do have an assembly slot, be sure to find out how long it should last, as well as making it as creative as you can – you want something to whet the children's appetites.

Encourage your own church family to be thinking about who they can pass information to and invite along. Ask them, too, to be praying for the event. Producing prayer cards or bookmarks will help them remember to pray before, during and after *Epic Explorers*. Ask them to pray for:

• The preparation of the talks – that they will be clear, faithful, engaging and challenging.

• The leaders – that they will prepare well, and lead with wisdom and integrity.

• The children – that many will attend and that God, by his Spirit, will unveil their eyes to see who Jesus is and their need of a Saviour.

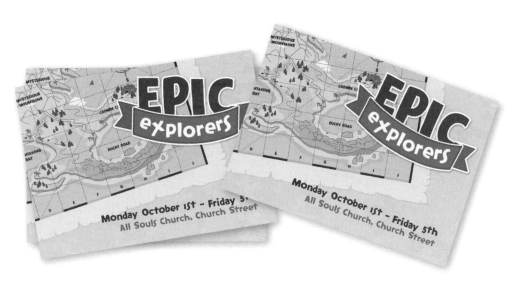

Team recruitment and roles

RECRUITMENT

The team you recruit is an essential part of the work. All the team should be Christians. Those who are running discussion groups should be able to teach clearly, faithfully and simply, to generate conversations, and to show compassion to those in their care. They should have a good grasp of Scripture and a desire to prepare well. You could put less-experienced leaders in with them, as a training ground.

Epic Explorers is a brilliant chance to cultivate and develop the gifts and skills of the teenagers within your church, as they serve in a supervised environment. They do not count however as adult leaders for your ratio, and it's good to make sure you have enough adults to mentor and nurture them.

The minimum recommended adult-to-child ratios are as follows:

- 1:8 – for children aged three-eight years.

- 1:8 for the first eight children, followed by 1:12 – for children aged eight and over.

There should always be more than one adult for any group.

Before you start recruiting your team, make sure you have looked through your church's child protection policy. All leaders involved should fill in and sign a confidential declaration form stating whether or not they have been the subject of criminal or civil proceedings, and whether they have caused harm to any child or put them at risk. There is a sample form, suitable for use in the UK, on page 32.

Emphasise to your team that this is the requirement of legal best-practice but that in addition, as Christians, we should respect the law of the land (Titus 3:1), we should be above reproach (1 Timothy 3:7), and our willingness to be checked is part of our commitment to care for the children.

If anyone gives an answer that causes concern, allow him or her to explain this disclosure personally. If you are in any doubt, consult your church leader. You may also find it useful to ask for a brief reference as part of the process, in which you ask abut the suitability of the potential team member and any concerns the referee may have. Ensure that confidentiality is maintained throughout.

ESSENTIAL ROLES

Running *Epic Explorers* will provide a unique opportunity to bring together people of different ages and stages who haven't served together before. Within the team, there will be a whole range of roles that need filling.

It is not essential that all the workers are experienced children's workers, for many others in your church will be more than able to help in the kitchen, on registration and in other background areas. Many others will be capable of running small-group sessions after some initial basic training. Serving together is a fantastic way of developing relationships within the church and allowing different people's gifts to be used, including teenagers.

Here are the roles you will need to delegate, if you are running a holiday club or vacation Bible school. There is an optional form on page 34 that may help you if you are recruiting a large team.

◼ Planning team

Put together a small team of people to help co-ordinate the week. The team should include experienced leaders with a range of skills and who represent different sections of the church family.

◼ Leaders-in-charge / Team captains

These people co-ordinate the up-front leading of the event and keep everything to time. They need to be enthusiastic, flexible yet aware of the session order, and authoritative.

◼ Small-group leaders

The role of the majority of the team is to sit among the children during the teaching sessions, to help enthuse and keep order. However, their key role is later as they accompany a small group of children in Bible discussion times, crafts and games sessions. They will have a great opportunity to get to know the children, have meaningful discussions about the teaching programme, and show the love of Christ in the way they act.

■ Musicians

You may want a small band to play with a range of instruments. Otherwise, you will need a couple of people who are confident singers to teach your songs to the children, using a CD.

■ Drama team

If you are including the *Epic Explorers* serial drama, you will need a small team of five budding actors (see page 148). These people need to be confident in front of a crowd, know how to project their voice, be prepared to make a fool of themselves and willing to learn their lines. They will need to set aside additional time for rehearsals and sorting props.

■ Registration team

This team will be responsible for ensuring every child is registered and welcomed, as well as seeking to build links with the parents/guardians. You may also allocate one of them to stay at the desk throughout the event to keep an eye on latecomers, site security and the collection of the children at the end of the event.

A register also needs to be kept of the leaders present. In the UK, these records must be retained for seven years.

■ Refreshment team

The team is responsible for preparing the refreshments for the children (and families if you are running something for parents also); checking with the registration team if any children have food allergies; and tidying up after the refreshments have been distributed.

■ First aider

Appoint at least one member of your team to be the official first aider. These people will need a current first-aid certificate and access to the first-aid kit. Kept with the first-aid kit should be an accident/incident book. It is essential that records be kept. The accident/incident should be recorded, however minor, along with the details on any action taken.

Make sure all the team know who the first aider is, along with any emergency procedures.

NON-ESSENTIAL ROLES

■ Kit man

This person will be responsible for setting up any TV, projector equipment and public-address system that is required.

■ Craft team/person

While most of the team will help out in their allocated age group's craft time, you may find it useful to appoint someone to be responsible for planning the craft activities, and making sure all the resources needed are in the correct place, at the correct time.

■ Timekeeper

This person needs to sit towards the front and hold up time signs to show these leading how long there is to go. They also play an essential role when group work is going on as they enable everyone to work in tandem.

■ Scorekeepers

Keep track of any points awarded.

■ Point givers

Points can be used as incentives. Children can be awarded them for sitting quietly, answering a question, singing enthusiastically etc. If they are used, it is important to make sure lots are distributed evenly by those sat among the children.

Theme and Setting

Epic Explorers, as the name suggests, has an exploration theme. Transform your venue into an adventure island, complete with sea, sand, palm trees, tropical birds and a number of destinations. The theme is picked up in different ways:

- The set can be tied into the teaching as you move from Breathtaking Bay and Discovery Dens to the Rocky road, via the Mysterious Mountains and Crown Cave.

- Through exploration games, crafts and activities.

- The serial drama is based around five children exploring Adventure Island.

Decorating your venue will help generate an exciting atmosphere and inspire the children's imaginations. You will need to think about how you can create the island, through the use of a variety of material. Consider what you can hang from the ceiling, what can be constructed and how you can cover the walls and floor. Building a set is a great way of drawing in other members of the church family, whether it is in donating resources or using their various gifts to produce props.

Here are some ideas for transforming your venue into an adventure island:

WALLS

Cover the back walls with sheets or strips of lining paper stuck together, which have been painted to look like the sea and sky. Make clouds by sticking on cotton wool. Alternatively, there are a number of sea and sky scene setters available on the internet (search for "sea scene setter").

FLOOR

Have the floor of the stage (or front of the room you're meeting in) covered in sandy-coloured material; or paint card a golden colour and sprinkle sand on while the paint is still wet. This can create your beach. A sandpit full of sand would also be useful for some of the challenges.

BREATHTAKING BAY

At the front of the stage/room, you could lay some wooden pallets flat for a jetty and then to one side have a blue tarpaulin on the floor. See if someone can lend you an inflatable dingy or rowing boat to put on the tarpaulin. Otherwise, why not have some fishing nets hanging off the pallet and onto the tarpaulin? You could even have a paddling pool filled with water near the jetty..

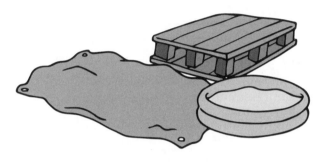

DISCOVERY DENS

Purchase some large MDF sheets and paint a Bible-time house on them.

Another suggestion is that you build a shack. This could be done by wrapping several grass skirts around the edge of a small table, or by placing pieces of driftwood vertically around the table. Then attach either tall bamboo canes (6 ft / 2 m) or wooden poles to the table legs. For the roof of the shack, you could cover a large sheet of cardboard with gardening raffia or straw. Two tika torches could go in front of the shack and paper lei flowers around the frame.

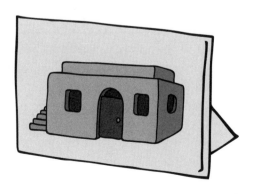

MYSTERIOUS MOUNTAINS

A stepladder covered in fabric makes a great mountain! You could sponge paint the fabric first in different shades of grey to make it look more rock-like. Use snow spray for the mountain peak.

You can add to the mountainous area by painting mountains on a backdrop, or cutting large triangles out of different coloured paper or fabric (grey, purple and green) and sticking them on a bed sheet

Stand artificial Christmas trees by the mountains to further the alpine affect.

CROWN CAVE

Borrow a dome tent and cover it in grey fabric to make the cave. To create grass to go nearby, cut triangles out of a long rectangular piece of heavy-weight card/card stock and paint it green. Place some plants around the cave area so it looks a little like a garden area.

Why not make this into a prize area and light up the inside with fairy lights to make it look out of the ordinary?

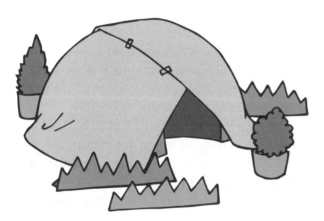

ROCKY ROAD

Make papier-mâché rocks of varying sizes by stuffing different plastic bags (from ordinary carrier bags to large refuse bags) with wads of newspaper. Then make a gluey-paste out of flour and water, and stick on strips of newspaper. You will probably need two-three coats. After the papier-mâché has dried, paint the rocks.

PALM TREES

Use carpet rolls as the bases for palm trees and cover in crumpled brown paper, or plastic plant pots stacked small end to small end, large to large.

Make palm branches out of green construction paper and wire or green garden canes.

WATERFALL

Paint large sheets of card/card stock or foam board to create the cliffs on either side of the waterfall. Have a garden cane run between the two, and from the cane hang long, thin strips of blue fabric, varying in shades. Then add some blue, silver or pearly shimmer door curtains on top and lay tulle fabric over it all to create the waterfall-like appearance. Place blue or clear fairy lights underneath. You could also put a fan behind if you want to add movement to the "water".

Have the waterfall flowing into a paddling pool, covered in blue cellophane. Use foam insulation and cushion stuffing to create the froth at the bottom.

You could make extra papier-mâché rocks to surround the pool.

JUNGLE AREA

Hang a cargo net and fill it with tissue paper tropical flowers. Make vines to add to the net out of green paper streamers.

Birds of paradise hanging from the ceiling, using fishing wire look effective. It's also possible to purchase inflatable monkeys and other tropical animals.

See www.ceministries.org/epic for more ideas for decorating your venue.

After Epic Explorers

Follow-up is a vital part of *Epic Explorers* as the five sessions should not be in isolation. It is good to think through what you can do for the children who have heard the gospel and built relationships with you. How can you encourage them to come along more regularly to children's groups within your church? Are there ways they can keep exploring? What support will you offer to those who have made a commitment? The following ideas aim to assist you continue the work you have begun.

1. Feedback forms

Feedback forms given out in the final session are a helpful way of encouraging the children to reflect on the things they've learned and what they now believe. Their comments will help guide how you can best follow them up. Make sure you have some good evangelistic booklets to pass on, as well as some basic Bible-reading notes.

As well as feedback forms for the children, there is also a form for parents of those attending an *Epic Explorer* holiday club or vacation Bible school. It will help the planning of future events and provide the parents with an opportunity to find out more themselves.

There are example forms available to download from www.ceministries.org/epic

2. Midweek clubs

An ideal way to maintain contact with the children is to encourage them to attend a midweek club in your church or your regular Sunday programme. Have information available during *Epic Explorers* so that you can advertise it. Make sure your team know what happens in each group and when the group meets.

You could make a short video to promote the groups, and have it playing each session as the children are dropped off and collected.

3. Activity days

Activity days throughout the year are a good way of renewing contact with the children. You could make them seasonal events, using something like *One Day Wonders* (The Good Book Company) or there is enough material in *Epic Explorers* to run another themed day.

Another way of continuing the "explorers" theme is to take the children on an expedition. A trip, whether it is a few hours or a whole day, is an excellent way of further developing relationships. Popular destinations are zoos, water parks, farms and soft play.

4. Family Events

It's important to remember that, through *Epic Explorers*, it's hoped whole families will be reached. It takes time to develop good relationships, so in your follow-up plan include something you can invite parents along to.

You could use another of the family events in *Epic Explorers*, take a selection of the games and challenges to plan a number of side stalls for families to rotate around, or organise a quiz night.

5. Pray

After *Epic Explorers*, keep praying for the children in your group. For those who have made a commitment, pray that they will grow and bear fruit. For those who are yet to make a commitment, ask God to work in their hearts and show them their need of a Saviour. Keep praying for yourself and the rest of the team, that you will keep trusting in God's timing and God's ways, and that you will be faithful in your follow-up.

6. Plan another *Epic Explorers*

It may be that you cannot re-run *Epic Explorers* in the same format right away, particularly if you have run it as a holiday club or vacation Bible school. However, there is enough material for you to run one of the other options. Plan in when you can do that, while the memory of it is still strong in the children's minds and they are keen to invite others along.

Confidential Declaration Form

In the UK, guidelines from the Home Office following the Children Act 1989 advise that all voluntary organisations, including churches, take steps to safeguard the children who are in their care. You are therefore asked to make the following declarations.

Because of the nature of the work for which you are applying, this post is exempt from the provision of section 4(ii) of the Rehabilitation of Offenders Act 1974, by virtue of the Rehabilitation of Offenders Act 1974 (exemptions) Orders 1975, and you are therefore not entitled to withhold information about convictions which, for other purposes, are "spent" under the provisions of the Act. In the event of an appointment, any failure to disclose such convictions could result in the withdrawal of approval to work with children in the church.

Do you have any current or spent criminal convictions, cautions, bindovers or cases pending?

Yes   No

Have you ever been held liable by a court under the Rehabilitation of Offenders Act 1974 for a civil wrong, or had an order made against you by a matrimonial or family court?

Yes   No

Has your conduct ever caused, or been likely to harm a child or put a child at risk, or, to your knowledge, has it ever been alleged that your conduct has resulted in any of these things?

Yes   No

Signed _____   Date _____

Referee's Name:

Referee's Address:

Referee's Telephone: Referee's Email:

Registration and Parental Consent Form

Name of child _____   Date of birth _____

Name of child _____   Date of birth _____

Name of child _____   Date of birth _____

Address:

Postcode / Zip code:

Email:

Phone: Mobile / Cell phone:

Name(s) of parent / guardian:

School your child attends:

Please give details of any health problems, medical conditions or allergies affecting your child, or any medication that they may be taking.

Please give any other information that you think may be useful to us in caring for your child:

To be read and signed by a parent / guardian:

☐ I give permission for my son / daughter to take part. I understand that leaders will take all reasonable care during the club, but I acknowledge the possibility that my child, for a short time, may be out of sight of a leader during the club time. I understand that personal accident insurance is my responsibility. I give permission for emergency medical treatment to be carried out in the event that I cannot be contacted.

☐ I am happy for my details to be kept on a church database, to be informed of other events.

☐ I give permission for photographs / video to be taken of my child for internal use only.

Signed _____   Date _____

Join the Epic Explorers team

Name:

Email: Phone:

What would you like to be involved in during *Epic Explorers*?	Yes	No	Would you like training/help?
Setting up daily			
Making resources / props			
Leading up-front			
Registration			
Welcoming			
Collect sheets / points			
Sound			
PowerPoint operator			
Scorekeeper			
Timekeeper			
Photographer			
Teaching Bible memory verse			
Running a quiz			
Helping with a quiz			
Music group			
Drama group			
Running games for 4-7s			
Running games for 8-11s			
Helping with games for 4-7s			
Helping with games for 8-11s			
Planning and organising crafts			
Helping with crafts for 4-7s			
Helping with crafts for 8-11s			
Refreshments			
Parents' coffee time			
First-aider			
Cleaning			
Team refreshments			
Family event			
Prayer events / keeping church informed			

Any other comments:

Please return this form to:

Team training session one

➡ Note: It is really important to meet with your team in the weeks leading up to Epic Explorers, to run through the aims, session format and content, provide basic training, and pray together.

ON ARRIVAL

As people arrive, have refreshments available. If you are running *Epic Explorers* as a holiday club or vacation Bible school, you may want to have the theme song playing in the background (see page 150).

GETTING GOING

Welcome the team and have them introduce themselves. You may want to run a short ice-breaker if it's a team who don't know one another particularly well.

It would also be good to share a brief devotional thought, reminding the team of God's rescue plan.

AIMS OF EPIC EXPLORERS

Explain that the general aim of *Epic Explorers* is to share the good news of Jesus with children and families in the area. Then add your own specific aims.

Ask the team to chat in smaller groups about how they think these aims will affect the way you plan and prepare; the way you run *Epic Explorers*; and the way you follow up children and families afterwards. You may want to give them a copy of the concentric circle diagram on page 22 (downloadable from www.ceministries.org/epic). Use this to help your team identify who you are mainly seeking to reach and where you hope, with God's grace, they will be at the end of the sessions. It would also be good to discuss how *Epic Explorers* fits into the bigger picture of church/organisation ministry and evangelism.

Discussing the aims will help give the team unity and ownership, as well as clarity.

TEACHING OVERVIEW: IDENTITY, MISSION AND CALL IN MARK'S GOSPEL

Give out a copy of the teaching programme timetable on page 9 (downloadable from www.ceministries.org/epic).

Explain that *Epic Explorers* has five teaching sessions based on Mark's Gospel. During these sessions the children will explore three major themes of Mark:

- **Who Jesus is** (his *identity*)
- **Why Jesus came** (his *mission*)
- **What it means to follow him** (his *call*)

These three themes are woven through every chapter of the book, although the first half of Mark (Mark 1:1 – 8:30) is largely concerned with the question of Jesus' *identity*; and the second half with his *mission*.

The first half of Mark is bookended with statements on who Jesus is. It begins with: *"The beginning of the good news about Jesus the Messiah, the Son of God"* (Mark 1:1) and ends with Peter's declaration: *"You are the Messiah"* (Mark 8:29). In-between these bookends are accounts of Jesus' authority in his teaching and his miracles, which reveal his *identity*. During *Epic Explorers*, the children will look at two such accounts in Mark 1 and 2, and they will begin to gather evidence proving Jesus is God's Son. Mark 2 will also raise the question of why Jesus came, as our sin problem and need for forgiveness is highlighted.

The cross dominates **the second half of Mark's Gospel**. Three times, Jesus predicts his death and resurrection, and from Mark 11 onwards, the anticipation is mounting as Jesus enters Jerusalem. In these chapters, the reader is helped to see more clearly the purpose of Jesus' rescue *mission*: he had to suffer, die and rise again so that we could be forgiven by God and reconciled with him forever. The *Epic Explorers* will discover this as they look at Mark 15 and 16 in sessions 3 and 4.

The passage containing the turning point in the Gospel (Mark 8:27-38) has all three themes of *identity*, *mission* and *call* in quick succession. This passage will be used for the final session to summarise *who Jesus is* and *why he came*, before considering *what it means to follow him*.

Give your team time to look over the timetable and ask any questions they have regarding the teaching content.

CORE COMPONENTS

Run through the core components of the course with your team:

Introductory activities

These are designed to tie in with the theme of session. It is important that they don't dominate or take up too much time, but rather are integrated into everything else in the session. Everyone (leaders included) should join in.

Leaders may also need reminding to explain afterwards the link between the activity and the rest of the session, as children won't automatically join up the dots.

Teaching

The talk will be around 10 minutes. It should be clearly and visually presented. Remind team members that they need to be listening attentively and encouraging the children to do the same.

Discussion groups

These provide an opportunity to consider the Bible passage further with the children, using the *Epic Logbook* (8-11s) and *Scratch Pad* (4-7s). There are leaders' notes to help generate the conversation and assist with explanations. Leaders should aim to speak less than the children, and should encourage the children to ask questions. More training will be giving on leading these groups next time.

THE FORMAT AND TIMINGS FOR YOUR EPIC EXPLORERS

Use the appropriate outline (pages 13-19) to show your team how your *Epic Explorers* programme will fit together, including a family event if you're having one. You may also want to explain the exploration theme a little if you are running a holiday club or vacation Bible school.

QUESTIONS

Give opportunity for your team to ask questions about the core components and other elements of the programme.

SET PREPARATION FOR NEXT TIME

Ask everyone to read through Mark's Gospel three or four times (each read-through will probably take about an hour) before the next training session. Encourage them to pick out the *identity*, *mission* and *call* themes.

PRAYER

Spend some time praying in groups for one another, that you will:

• Prepare well and be dependant upon God.

• Work well together and show that you are Jesus' disciples by your love for one another.

• Teach and lead faithfully.

Pray too that:

• Children will come along and the Holy Spirit will open their eyes.

• The practicalities will come together well.

Team training session two

ON ARRIVAL

As people arrive, have refreshments available. If you are running *Epic Explorers* as a holiday club or vacation Bible school, you may want to have the theme song playing in the background (see page 150).

GETTING GOING

Welcome back the team. You may want to run another short ice-breaker if it's a team who don't know one another particularly well.

It would also be good to share a brief devotional thought from Mark's Gospel or ask them what things struck them as they read through Mark.

DISCUSSION GROUPS

Why have discussion groups?

- They reinforce the teaching. Questions are asked more easily and things explored more deeply. They can help with application and give children the opportunity to respond.

- They are relational. Consistent discussion groups encourage deeper trust levels and, with everyone involved, children are more likely to be open and honest. Discussion groups also give leaders a chance to share from their own life, and understand the joys and struggles of those in their care.

- They are also an opportunity to train and learn from one another.

The setting

- Check how much time you have and plan what you have to do in that time.

- Remove distractions beforehand.

- Sit in a circle and make sure everyone is comfortable.

- Sit troublesome children either opposite you so that you can see what is going on, or next to you.

- You should sit facing anything that is distracting (such as other groups) so that the children have their backs to it.

- Use eye contact and body language to help you engage the children.

Introduction

- Remember children's names and what they say. React and interact (even jot it down so you can use it in examples in other sessions or to chat to them further).

- If there's time, have a brief opening item that will relax people, eg: joke; light-hearted question (eg: describe favourite ice-cream); game (eg: give 2 truths, 1 lie – can they spot which is the lie?); introduce the person next to you. This will loosen tongues and encourage the children to relax.

ASKING QUESTIONS

Run through the chart on page 38. Then, in twos or threes, ask the leaders to pick out something they struggle with regards to discussion groups and chat about things that may help (if time, pray about this together).

Running discussion groups

DOs	DON'Ts
Do prepare and pray (for individuals as well as the Bible study).	**Don't** be afraid to ask for help
Do ask questions that deal with feelings as well as facts eg: "How do you feel?"	**Don't** ask yes / no questions. Rather, encourage discussions.
Do encourage honesty always – including by example, sharing your own life.	**Don't** dismiss any contributions. Praise people for their contribution even if it isn't quite what you were looking for.
Do be a good listener • *Reflect:* "It sounds like...", "You mean...", "So you want to..." • *Reaffirm:* "That's pretty important to you", "That must be difficult for you" • *Request:* "Tell me a bit more about that", "So what happened then?", "How did you feel?"	**Don't** do all the talking. If a child asks you a question, first ask them what they understand before you answer. Encourage others in the group to answer.
Do ask questions that are relevant and at the right level.	**Don't** assume knowledge and don't use lots of Christian jargon.
Do follow up responses with more questions, and encourage others in the group to do the same. Be willing to challenge if appropriate.	**Don't** feel you have to answer everything.
Do be flexible eg: if it's a quiet group, then you could break it down into paired discussions and then ask the pairs to feed back.	**Don't** be afraid of silence – rather interpret it. Is the question too simple? Can you break down into smaller questions? Have you asked too many questions? Are they thinking or are they bored?
Do use illustrations eg: own life example, scenarios, quotes, pictures.	**Don't** forget there are different learning styles so be creative eg: application sketch, what happens next..., quiz, write a rap or chant or song, draw a picture, listen to music, film clip (but make sure you are supporting and teaching your main aim).

COPING WITH DIFFERENT PERSONALITIES

Within the discussion groups there will be a number of different personalities. Run through the characters below and briefly comment on the top tips for how best to handle them. Ask people to add further suggestions as you do so.

◼ Chatterbox Charlie

Very talkative and dominates discussions.

- Sit next to "Charlie" to reduce eye contact.

- Ask: "What does someone else think?"

- Ask "Charlie" to summarize the discussions, so that he has to listen to the others' contributions.

- Talk to him privately about the problem.

- If you have lots of "Chatterbox Charlies", then have an item that group members must hold, or cards they must hand in, before they can speak.

◼ Debater Dani

Always presents opposition, and challenges every point.

- It can be intimidating for others but at the same time can help produce a "proper" discussion – so aim to direct "Dani" rather than shut her up!

- Ask for other suggestions.

- Break into pairs so that everyone has the chance to express a viewpoint.

- Set a group rule that it's ok to disagree but you can't talk over each other and can't put down those with different ideas.

- Make sure you stick to main point – have a question time towards the end of *Epic Explorers*.

◼ Voiceless Vic

Quieter and rarely contributes.

- Try to get to know "Vic". His silence could be because he is shy or because he doesn't want to be there or because he doesn't understand. Equally, he may be a heavily "auditory" learner, and will learn without having to contribute.

- Give "Vic" chances by asking: "Does anyone want to add anything?" Direct questions sometimes help.

- Sit opposite "Vic" to maximise eye contact.

- Take time to chat outside the discussion group and learn interests, so you can "pitch" questions and illustrations that interest him.

- Personal encouragement can make all the difference – both outside of group time and in thanking him for contributions.

◼ Crisis Christine

Wants attention and for everyone to know what they are dealing with all the time.

- "Christine" only really contributes to talk about herself or make negative contributions, rather than actually responding to other's answers – so chat to her beforehand to hear her "crisis" or say we'll pray for one another at the end.

- Help "Christine" see that the group is there to help others, not just herself.

- If there is a genuine crisis, then be willing to chat about it there/aside and to ditch what was planned.

◼ Distracter Dom

Constantly fidgeting and prone to sidetracking.

- If "Dom" is a fidget, persistently stifling him will only prove negative, so try to direct his energies eg: being the scribe, holding something up…

- If it's a "red herring" he are distracting with, say: "Can we follow that one up later? What about the question we were asking?"

- If "Dom" tells a joke, join in but then bring the group back to the discussion. With misplaced humour, ignore the comments and move the discussion on.

- Try to do some active learning with the group, so you're not just talking every week. At least they'll stop you settling for boring Bible studies!

◼ Churchy Casey

Knows all the answers instantly.

- Remember that "Casey's" knowledge may not indicate spiritual depth and that "church kids" can be the hardest to reach. Conversely, there will be some who are committed believers and will give the "right" answer because it is true for them.

- Don't settle for pat answers – either ask why, or give the opposite answer to get "Casey" to think through her opinions.

- Ask "Casey" to help you with questions so that she engages with the text.

- Scenarios can help the children think through how they usually react and how they can relevantly apply the passage.

Now split your leaders into groups of four or five and ask them to complete the group exercise below, referring back to the top tips. They could also use the DOs and DON'Ts table on page 38 to help them.

The group exercise can also be downloaded from www.ceministries.org/epic

Group exercise

You have a small group to run. There are six young people in your group:

- one is a non-church child who is totally disinterested.

- one is a non-church child who is showing real interest and is asking questions.

- one is a church child who does not volunteer to contribute to the discussion.

- one is a child from a church family who fidgets constantly and has already destroyed his pen.

- one knows all the answers and replies before anyone else has a chance to speak.

- one talks loudly over everyone else about irrelevant stuff, and seems particularly interested in drawing the attention of the children in the next group.

What do you do with your group?

Think about:

■ Who do you think is the key person to deal with? How?

■ What is your tactic for dealing with those who aren't engaging? How about those who are engaging too much?

■ How do you try to get some balance so that everyone has a chance to engage?

■ How could you make sure you are prepared for the same group again in the next session?

USING THE BOOKLETS

Spend some time looking over the *Epic Logbook* (8-11s) and *Scratch Pad* (4-7s), considering how best you will use them to assist discussions.

SET PREPARATION FOR NEXT TIME

Ask everyone to prepare the discussion group material for session one.

PRAYER

Have people pray with those they are leading discussion groups with. Pray that you will:

- Plan your discussion times prayerfully and carefully.

- Spur one another on.

- Have great wisdom, patience, kindness and enthusiasm.

Pray too that:

- Children will come along and the Holy Spirit will open their eyes.

- The practicalities will come together well.

Further training

If you are running an Epic Explorers *holiday club or vacation Bible school, you may want to run an additional training session, which includes the following.*

THE LEGAL STUFF

Talk through the guidelines for child protection (summarize your church/organisation policy), health and safety and emergency procedures.

DIFFERENT TEAM ROLES

Explain the different roles within the team, and some basic principles for running games, teaching the memory verse and asking quiz questions.

If you have different teams eg: crafts team or a band, give them opportunity to talk together or ask the co-ordinators of these groups to pass on any information needed.

BEHAVIOUR MANAGEMENT

Good discipline creates a truly relaxed, enjoyable and reverent environment within which we can practically communicate the message of the gospel, both through our own Christ-like actions and through the material we teach. Good relationships and clear expectations are at the heart of loving, effective discipline.

It may be useful to have a signal or set phrase with accompanying action, that your team members can use when you want the children to stop what they are doing and be silent.

In addition, a step-by-step approach to behaviour management can help, both when the children are altogether and in smaller activity groups. For example:

1. **Watch for the children that wind others up and intervene before there is a problem.** Make intervention precise and clear, eg: "spread out and look out"—sitting among a group or separating certain groups of children.

2. **Try to use implicit cues** (ie: body language and eye contact) first. Always consider how, why and when you need to draw attention to misbehaviour.

3. **Speak to individuals discreetly.** Be quiet, firm, precise and brief. Explain why they have not reached your expectations.

4. If the child alters their behaviour for the better, respond positively. If they do not, **offer the child a choice of improving their behaviour or taking time out**. Avoid threats you cannot carry out.

5. **If time out is taken, child to be seated for five minutes in lobby, with the worker** (ideally, out of sight of the other children, but make sure you can be seen by at least one other team member).

   While there **hold a brief discussion as to what is at the heart of the problem**, ie: get beyond the behaviour. Use this to teach about repentance, eg: "If you come back and say sorry, then all will be forgiven and forgotten. We love you but your behaviour is unacceptable". Tailor your reprimand to the individual and occasion. **Note the date, child's name and behaviour in the incident book** (kept with the registration material).

6. **If a child has time out twice in the event**, their parents should be contacted.

Note: Remember to adapt to those with special needs eg: educational, behavioural or medical needs.

Leader's Guide

Introduction

Epic Explorers is designed so that you will have all you need to run a holiday club or vacation Bible school, a short series in a weekly club, or a children's *Christianity Explored* course.

- You will find **outlines for the five sessions**, with a wide range of activities to support the teaching theme for each one.

- There are also **two talk outlines for each session**, one for a group of 4-11s all together (eg: in a holiday club or vacation Bible school), and one for a group of 8-11s only (eg: in a weekly club or course).

▨ *Note: We do not recommend using* Epic Explorers *just with 4-7s as the material has not been designed to use in this way.*

There is a strong exploration theme throughout as the children discover the different places on Adventure Island. There is a **selection of Exploration crafts, games and quiz ideas** starting on page 47. These can be used in any of the five sessions.

You will also find **specific activity ideas for each session**, along with **help in using the two children's booklets:** the *Epic Logbook* (8-11s) and *Epic Scratch Pad* (4-7s).

We have designed this material to be as flexible as possible so that you can plan *Epic Explorers* to suit your particular group or situation. You will find some suggested programme outlines on pages 13-19 in Section 1 of this Leader's Guide.

However, you know your group best, so you may want to make some changes to these outlines if they would suit your group better.

Page	Section	Contents
47	Exploration crafts, games and quiz ideas	*A range of activities that pick up the theme of exploring Adventure Island. These can be used in any of the five sessions.*
55	Session 1: Breathtaking Bay	• *Jesus is God's Son (Mark 1:1, 16-34)*
69	Session 2: Discovery Dens	• *Jesus forgives sins (Mark 2:1-17)*
85	Session 3: Mysterious Mountains	• *Jesus died in our place (Mark 15)*
101	Session 4: Crown Cave	• *Jesus is alive and offers new life (Mark 16:1-8)*
117	Session 5: Rocky Road	• *Following Jesus (Mark 8:27-35)*
135	Family events (at the end of a club/course)	*Outlines for a Family service to close a holiday club or vacation Bible school; or a Family treasure hunt or fun night that can be held in an evening or weekend at the end of a course. Includes talk outlines to sum up the teaching from all five passages.*

Exploration crafts, games and quiz ideas

EXPLORATION CRAFTS

 Binoculars

You will need:
- Cardboard cylinders (eg: the insides of kitchen-paper rolls)
- Thin, black sticky tape
- Ribbon or cord
- Black, dark green, light green, medium green, brown and yellow paint
- Paint brushes
- Water
- Hole punch
- Double-sided sticky tape

1. Stick the two cylinders together using double-sided tape. You may want to make a smaller cylinder out of card (card stock) to go between the two tubes.

2. Stick black tape around the bottom and top of the cylinders.

3. Hole punch each side of the binoculars, close to one end.

4. Paint the binoculars in a camouflage style.

5. Thread the cord/ribbon through one hole, tie a knot on the inside to hold in place, and thread through the other hole. Knot this end on the inside as well.

 Expedition bottles

You will need:
- Plastic water bottles
- Permanent marker pens
- Glass pens or OHT pens

1. Give each child a water bottle.

2. Ask them to write their name on it somewhere using a glass pen or permanent marker.

3. Use the pens to create their own design. Don't touch the design until it is dry!

 Expedition hats

You will need:
- Sun visors or spiral hats (available from Baker Ross in the UK and Oriental Trading in the US)
- Felt-tip pens
- Funky-foam letters
- Stickers
- Glitter glue

1. Hand out the visors/hats.

2. Ask the children to colour and personalize them by decorating, eg: following the swirls, spelling their name.

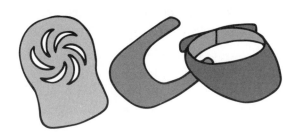

Explorer pom-pom bugs

You need:
- Pom-poms of varying sizes
- Googly eyes
- Pipe cleaners
- PVA (white) glue
- Glue spreaders
- Scissors

Dragonflies

1. Cut a pipe cleaner in half, and place the pieces side by side. This will give the base for the dragonfly's body.

2. Curl the top of the two pipe cleaners to make them look like antennae.

3. Take two more pipe cleaners and make them loop into wing shapes. Twist them together; then twist them onto the middle of the dragonfly's body.

4. Glue five or six small pom-poms onto the two pipe cleaners that form the body.

5. Stick googly eyes onto the top pom-pom.

Creepy crawlies

1. Cut one pipe cleaner into 6 or 8 (depending on how many legs you want the creature to have!).

2. Glue a small pom-pom to a larger one.

3. Stick two googly eyes on the smaller pom-pom.

4. Bend the bottom of the pipe cleaners to create feet. Bend the top of the pipe cleaner also if you want the creepy crawly to have knees.

5. Glue your legs onto the pom-pom.

Flags

You will need:
- Felt-tip pens
- Art straws or small garden canes
- Sticky tape
- Scissors
- Card (card stock) A5/half US letter

1. Ask the children to design a flag for their newly-discovered land.

2. Colour using felt-tip pens.

3. When finished, tape the flag to the top of the art straw or garden cane.

Maps

Note: This craft will need to be done over two days.

You will need:
- Paper
- Tea bags in warm (not hot) water
- Felt-tip pens
- Ribbon

Day 1

1. Rip the edges from the paper so it has jagged sides.

2. Crumple the paper up into a ball.

3. Flatten out the paper.

4. Take a tea bag, soak it in warm water, and then wipe it all over the paper. Soak the tea bag in water again if it dries out.

5. Leave the paper to dry (and maybe do another short craft, eg: the expedition bottle, as the map could then go inside it).

Day 2

1. Draw an island outline and put a big "x" somewhere on it.

2. Add a picture of a compass in the corner.

3. Draw the places we're travelling to in the week (Breathtaking Bay, Discovery Dens, Mysterious Mountains, Crown Cave and Rocky Road). Join them using a dotted-line trail that twists and turns.

4. Maybe add some more landmarks, eg: the Jungle of Doom, the Whispering Waterfalls, and Snake's Pass.

5. Roll up the map and tie with a ribbon.

Marshmallow world

You will need:
- Edible markers
- Marshmallows
- Toothpicks
- A large cake decorated as an island, or a cup cake per child

1. Give the children four marshmallows each.

2. Ask them to draw something on each marshmallow that they would like on their island, eg: a tree, a mountain, caves, etc.

3. When they have drawn their pictures, the children can stick each marshmallow on a toothpick, and then either place in their own miniature island or on the large cake island.

4. Have a look at all the places that have been created; then eat and enjoy!

Shooters

You will need:
- Plastic cups or yogurt pots
- Balloons
- Mini-marshmallows
- Scissors
- Stickers to decorate

1. Cut the bottom third off your cup or pot.

2. Tie a knot in the end the balloon; then cut off about 1cm / ½ inch from the other end.

3. Stretch the balloon over the top of the cup or pot (where the lip is).

4. Decorate the pot using stickers.

5. Put the mini-marshmallow inside the cup, on the knotted centre.

6. Point the cup away from people, pull back the outer knot and let go to fire the marshmallow. How many wild animals can they catch on this island?!

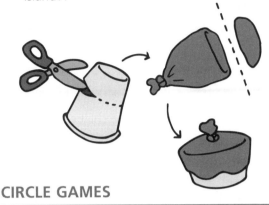

CIRCLE GAMES

Explore, explore, war!

(Based on "Duck, duck, goose".)

1. Children sit in a circle facing inwards.

2. One person is chosen as the explorer, who walks around the circle.

3. As they walk around, they tap people's heads and say either: "Explore" or "War".

4. When the explorer says "War", the person they tapped gets up and tries to chase the explorer around the circle.

5. The goal is to catch the explorer before they are able sit down in the "warrior's" spot.

6. If the warrior is not able to do this, they become the "explorer" for the next round and play continues.

Great explorers

(Based on "Fish in the sea".)

1. Children sit in a circle facing outwards and are named Armstrong, Dora, Livingstone or Columbus.

2. When their name is called, they have to walk round the outside of the circle (the island).

3. Call out instructions to change the speed and direction of the runners, eg:

49

Heading to base camp: children walk around the circle.

Spying out the land: children tiptoe around the circle.

Stuck in the bog: children hop around the circle.

Avalanche: children run quickly round the circle.

Enemies attack: children turn and run around the circle in the opposite direction.

All the explorers: all the children get up and go around the circle.

4. End each round by shouting: " Explorers go home". The last child to reach their place and sit down must face inwards. They could continue to play on the inside of the circle.

EXPLORATION GAMES

Pin the speedboat on the map

You will need:
- An island map (page 153)
- A blindfold
- A small speedboat to stick on (page 155)
- Blu-Tack reuseable adhesive

1. Blindfold a child and spin them around three times.

2. They have to try and stick the speedboat on "Breathtaking Bay".

3. The one who is closest wins.

Swampy eyeball fishing with feet

You will need:
- Paddling pool
- Bath jelly (trade name "Gelli Baff") to fill the paddling pool
- Marbles
- Small chairs
- Bowl of water
- Paper towels

1. Have the children sit round the edge of the paddling pool on chairs.

2. They have to place one foot each in the swamp; then fish out as many marbles as possible in the given time.

3. The winner is the person who catches the most.

4. Have a bowl of water for them to wash their feet in after.

The eating challenge

You will need:
- Grasshopper legs (Twiglet)
- Frog eye (peeled grape)
- Fly (raisin)
- Ants' blood (prune juice)
- Sardine
- Sheep dropping (black olive)
- Plants (spinach)
- Raw onion
- Cow's brain (feta cheese)
- Salami
- Piece of Mars bar
- Snake skin (astrobelt / fizzy strawberry belt)
- Gummy worms
- Mussels (check about seafood allergies)

1. A tray will be laid out with bits of food in three categories:

   One point – ok
   Two points – gross
   Three points – really gross

2. Place the tray on a chair. The children are to sit in a line a couple of metres back so they can't see what's on the tray until they get there.

3. The first child comes up to the tray and can choose which category they want to eat from. When they have chewed and swallowed,

award them the number of points that corresponds to what they ate.

Watch out, the explorer's about

You will need:
- Nerf guns (that fire foam darts)
- Toy animals, varying in sizes

1. Explain that explorers often have to catch their own food.

2. The children have to shoot the animals.

3. Award points, depending on what they shoot.

RELAY RACES

Expedition

You will need:
- Balloons
- Bucket
- Small flags on art straws or sticks

1. Divide the children into teams and line the teams up at one end of the room. At the other end of the room have a bucket with small flags in.

2. Within their team, the children are to get into pairs and stand back-to-back.

3. Sandwich a balloon between the first pair's backs.

4. They have to shuffle to the bucket. If a balloon pops or drops, they must go back to the start for a replacement.

5. When they arrive at the bucket, they need to pick a flag and march back to their team, carrying the balloon and the flag, before the next pair can go.

6. The team wins if their players are the first to all complete the expedition.

Exploring the island

You will need:
- Equipment to build an obstacle course, eg:
  - A paddling pool filled with water, and with fish made from plastic lids in it, labelled: "Breathtaking Bay"
  - Fishing nets by the side of Breathtaking Bay
  - Tables, labelled: "Discovery Dens"
  - An upturned laundry basket, labelled: "Mysterious Mountains"
  - A chair covered in a blanket, labelled: "Crown Cave"
  - A set of cones marking out the "Rocky Road" path

1. Divide the children into teams and have them line up.

2. One team member at a time has to complete the obstacle course by:
   - running to the paddling pool and catching a fish at Breathtaking Bay;
   - then climbing over the roof of Discovery Dens;
   - next, running round the mountain and crawling through the cave;
   - finally, weaving in and out of the cones on the Rocky Road.

3. Once one team member has completed the course, another one can start.

4. The winning team is the first to all complete the course.

Pan for gold

You will need:

- A sieve per team
- A paddling pool filled with sand
- Chocolate/plastic coins
- Some random small objects, eg: washers, dice

1. Divide the children into teams and have them in single-file lines at one end of the room. Put the paddling pool at the far end.

2. One child from each team is to run to the sand and use the sieve to find a treasure, by sifting the sand.

3. Once they have a coin, they can pick it out and run back to the team for the next person to go.

4. The winning team is the first team where each child has found a coin.

RUN-AROUND GAMES

Musical islands

You will need:

- Sheets of newspaper
- Music on a CD or MP3 player
- Sound system

1. Play this like musical chairs, only use pieces of newspaper in place of chairs on the floor. The children must walk around the paper "islands".

2. When the music stops, the children must stand on one of the "islands" or they're out. Only one child can stand on each "island".

3. Each time, remove a sheet of paper or two, until only one explorer remains.

Scavenger hunt

You will need:

- Lots of pictures of different explorer items (eg: passports, binoculars, compasses) hidden around the room.
- Write different point values on each picture, eg: 1 point for binoculars (easy to find), 3 points for a compass (not as easy to find), 5 points for a passport (fewer of them and difficult to find)

1. Explain to the children that they are to explore the room and find as many items as they can.

2. At the end of a set time, count up and see how many points they have won.

TEAM GAMES

Exploring the land

1. Divide the children into teams. Have each team stand in a line.

2. Give each person in the line a name, depending on their position in the line, eg: the first person in each line is "beach", the next is "mountain" and so on. These names can be explorers, animals on an island, or different locations on Adventure Island.

3. Make up an adventure story about exploring an island. Stand opposite the teams and tell the story.

4. Every time a player hears their name, they have to run to the storyteller and high-five them.

5. Note who high-fives first and award a point for that team.

QUIZ IDEAS

📌 *Note: For each quiz, prepare a range of questions based on the main teaching points and what has been covered in the session. Make sure the questions are clear and pitched at all ages.*

Epic explorer

Aims: To dress their representative leader up as an explorer; to reinforce what has been taught in a fun way; and to help teams score points.

You will need:
- Explorer costumes:
  - Explorer hats x 2
  - Binoculars x 2
  - Waistcoats x 2
  - Camouflage face paint
  - Backpacks x 2
  - Boots x 2 pairs
- Dice
- PowerPoint slide

1. Explain that: "It's important that explorers have the right kit so…"

2. Have two volunteer leaders to be dressed up. When a question is answered correctly, the child who answered comes and rolls the dice. Each number represents an item of clothing – make a PowerPoint slide showing which is which, eg: if you roll a "1", put on a hat.

3. If the team has not already rolled that number, the volunteer leader puts on the item of clothing. However, if the team who roll already have that item of clothing, the clothing goes to the other team (if they don't have it). The team with the most items of clothes at the end wins.

It can be good to get the teams chanting which number they want to roll.

Island trek

Aims: To move each team's leader from Breathtaking Bay around the island to reach Rocky Road; to reinforce what has been taught in a fun way; and to help teams score points.

You will need:
- PowerPoint or a scoreboard
- If you have a scoreboard, you will need numbers 1-16. Each number needs written underneath it either a "go", a "whoa" or a "no". You will need 8 x "go", 4 x "whoa" and 4 x "no"
- 2 volunteer leaders (maybe dressed in the explorer costumes), standing at the front
- Labelled places, if they are not part of the set design:
  - Breathtaking Bay
  - Discovery Dens
  - Mysterious Mountains
  - Crown Cave
  - Rocky Road

1. Explain that: "It's time to explore the island so…"

2. If a child gets a question right, they can choose a number on the PowerPoint/scoreboard.

3. Behind each number is one of three instructions:
   - **Go** – the leader takes one step forward
   - **Whoa** – the leader stays where they are
   - **Nooooooo** – the leader takes one step backwards

4. The winning team is the team whose leader moves the furthest.

It's good to get the teams chanting either "go" or "no".

Shooting practice

Aims: To squirt the balls off the cups; to reinforce what has been taught in a fun way; and to help teams score points.

You will need

- 5 plastic cups, turned upside down
- 5 table-tennis balls, placed on top of the cups
- A water pistol
- Tarpaulin

1. Explain that: "All good explorers need to do shooting practice to make sure they can catch food! So…"

2. When the children answer the question correctly, call them up to the front and give them ten seconds to squirt the water pistol at the balls, trying to shoot them off the cup.

   They score:
   – 20 points for one ball
   – 40 points for two balls
   – 60 points for three balls
   – 80 points for four balls
   – 100 points for five balls

3. The winning team is the team that scores the most points.

It's good to get the teams chanting either "hit" or "miss".

Bulking up!

Aims: To bulk up their leader as much as possible, with a belly full of sand(!); to reinforce what has been taught in a fun way; and to help teams score points.

You will need:

- Tub of sand
- Small bucket

1. Explain: "An explorer needs the strength to scramble up mountains, trek though forests and wade through swamps. They need the strength to sail the seven seas and conquer new lands. So let's get bulking up…"

2. Have two volunteer leaders with baggy vest tops/t-shirts on – which need to be tucked into their trousers. Have them posing like a strong man, with muscles flexed.

3. When a child gets the question right, they have ten seconds to transfer as much sand as possible from the tub to inside their representative leader's shirt, using a small bucket.

4. The winning team is the one who has the most bulked-up leader!

Get the children all shouting the countdown.

Victory is vine!

Aims: To end up with the longest vine; to reinforce what has been taught in a fun way; and to help teams score points.

You will need:

- Different lengths of green fabric (10cm-150cm / 4 inches - 60 inches), cut into thin strips, as vines
- A large plant pot with the vines inside. Hang 5cm of each vine over the top edge (so they all appear to be the same length)

1. Explain that: "Explorers love to swing and climb on vines, so who can make the longest one?"

2. When a child answers the question correctly, they can come up and pull a vine out of the pot. As their team collects more and more vines, tie them together.

3. At the end, compare the vines to see which team has the longest one.

Get the children shouting "whopper" or "midget".

BREATHTAKING BAY
Jesus is God's Son

Bible passage
Mark 1:1, 16-34

Main aims
- Children will know that Jesus has authority over everything.
- Children will understand that Jesus is God's Son.

Session options
The following pages include a wide variety of activities. See pages 14-19 for suggestions of which activities to choose for different contexts or length of time.

Notes for leaders
➡ *Read Mark 1:1-34*

Mark doesn't leave his readers hanging in suspense, but rather, gets straight to the point as to the purpose of his book. In verse 1, we see that Mark's Gospel is all about Jesus and the good news he brings as God's only chosen King and Son. The following verses give us further evidence as to who Jesus is and why he came – his *identity*, *mission* and *call*. Jesus is the promised one (verses 1-3), the superior one (verses 4-8), the eternal Son (verses 9-11), the one who does not give in to temptation (verses 12-13) and the one who offers forgiveness and life, under his rule (verses 14-15). And so comes the call to "repent and believe" in verse 15.

What we see in the rest of Mark 1 is that God's King has awesome authority, which he uses to build his kingdom. It's authority that has never been seen in such a way before (verses 22, 27-28, 37, 45).

First, we see the authority in Jesus' words and teaching. When Jesus summons Simon and Andrew to stop what they are doing and follow him in verse 17, and James and John in verses 19-20, they respond with immediate obedience. There's no delay or disagreement, but rather, a willingness to leave behind their families, work, security and possessions. Who can command men in such a way? Only God has the right to demand that we leave everything and follow him. It is part of his call when we repent and believe (Mark 8:34-38, 10:21).

We see another example of Jesus' authority as he teaches and releases people from Satan's kingdom, through his preaching of God's word (verses 21-28); even unclean spirits recognize Jesus' mission and are subject to his commands. The demons are right in their proclamations in verse 24, but not allowed to speak, as it was not time for Jesus' saving death. Jesus would reveal his identity in his time and way, not theirs. Note how people were amazed at his words, even before he drove the impure spirit out of the man, in verse 22 as well as verse 27.

Next, we see Jesus' authority over all types of sickness (verses 29-34), as he restores people's health, beginning with Simon Peter's mother-in-law. Her healing is immediate and absolute, and she is instantly able to serve others. As news spreads, and others are healed, so an entire city gathers to Jesus within a day (verse 33)! All this is a foretaste of what is to come when God's kingdom fully arrives – Jesus is Lord over everything and every-one; he will put an end to sickness and evil once and for all.

In the midst of a wave of excitement, Jesus does something very surprising – he withdraws to pray. He then shows that, rather than focusing on healing and his rising popularity, his priority is to preach the good news (verses 35-39).

Leader's prayer: Why not follow Jesus' example, and stop and pray now? Praise God that he is still in the business of calling people into his kingdom, releasing people from Satan's kingdom, and wanting to restore us to his likeness. Praise him for the work he has done in your life, and pray for those you will be working with in *Epic Explorers*. Ask God to keep you passionate about prayer and prioritizing sharing the Bible.

BREATHTAKING BAY: TALK IDEA 1

Suitable for a holiday club or vacation Bible school, ages 4-11 or 8-11

You will need:

- A crown
- The Island map visual
- The "Breathtaking Bay" coloured visual to stick up

This talk outline can also be downloaded from www.ceministries.org/epic

---

March on wearing a crown; then continue to march on the spot while barking out orders…

Attention! On your feet, right away and march. That's right, up two, up two, up two, up two. Now halt! Stretch up! Sit down! Salute! At ease.

Relax voice

Well done – brilliant obeying. But why did you do what I asked? (pause) **It was because I was in charge; I had power and authority** (flex muscles) **over you. I said something and it happened.**

Well, today's true story is all about the person with the most power and authority (flex muscles). **We find it in the New Testament part of the Bible** (hold up Bible). **Mark begins by telling us that Jesus** (crown shape) **has power and authority** (flex muscles) **over everything** (sweep arms in front of you) **because he is God's** (point up) **chosen King and Son. Then Mark gives loads of examples in the beginning of his book just to make sure we've got it.**

So we're going to go to Breathtaking Bay (point to on map) **to see what Jesus** (crown shape) **does. Every time I say "Jesus", I want you to make a crown shape; every time I say "authority", I want you to flex your arms; every time I say "God", I want you to point up; and every time I say "everything", I want you to sweep your arms in front of you.**

Give the children a chance to practise the actions as you say each of the four words.

Peter and his friends were getting ready to go on another fishing trip. It's what they did, day in, day out. Get the nets ready, sail out on

Lake Galilee, fish until they caught enough, then come back to shore to sell it. It was their job, their way of making money and surviving. But that was about to change. Forever. For that particular day was no ordinary day.

That particular day, Jesus (crown shape) **walked up to them on the sand and said: "Hey guys! Come on, leave everything and follow me! I've got plans for you to work with me."** Leave everything! Their family, their work, the lot. Do you know what they did? (pause) They dropped their nets on the beach, and they followed Jesus (crown shape). **All of them. Right away. No questions, no arguments.**

Peter and his friends could tell that Jesus (crown shape) **was important. They could see he had authority** (flex muscles) **over everything** (sweep arms in front of you) **just by the way he spoke. And so if Jesus** (crown shape) **said follow, they knew they had to follow.**

Well, they followed Jesus (crown shape) **to a place called Capernaum, where they listened to him teach about God** (point up) **and watched impossible things happen. They saw all sorts of ways that Jesus** (crown shape) **has authority** (flex muscles) **over everything** (sweep arms in front of you).

He knew more than anyone else. He could **make people better just like that** (click fingers), **even people who had evil spirits inside them. His power showed he was God's** (point up) **Son. Wow! Peter and his friends were amazed at Jesus'** (crown shape) **authority** (flex muscles) **and they weren't the only ones; everyone else was, too.**

And then, Peter suddenly had a thought (pause). **His mother-in-law was really ill. She had an awful fever, all hot, sticky and shaky. He could take Jesus** (crown shape) **to meet her, to help her** – and so that's what they did.

They left the synagogue and went to Peter's house. Jesus (crown shape) **went straight up to Peter's mother-in-law and took hold of her hand. As he did, God's** (point up) **power worked in her and made her better right away. She was even able to get up and cook. Jesus** (crown shape) **had healed her! It was amazing; it was awesome; it was EPIC!**

And she wasn't the only one Jesus (crown shape) **healed that night. As soon as the news spread, loads of ill people flocked to Peter's house. Jesus** (crown shape) **was able to heal them all – he even drove out some evil spirits, just like that** (click fingers)**!**

Jesus (crown shape) **really does have authority** (flex muscles) **over everything** (sweep arms in front of you). **He really is God's** (point up) **Son.**

Peter and his friends kept following Jesus (crown shape) **after that. As they watched and learned from him, they began to work out who Jesus** (crown shape) **is. They started to understand more and more that Jesus** (crown shape) **is God's** (point up) **chosen King and Son – not just a good man or a clever miracle worker.**

Stick "Breathtaking Bay" coloured section on the map.

I wonder, who do you think Jesus (crown shape) **is? Over the next few sessions, we're going to hear about some more of the fantastic things Jesus** (crown shape) **did and said, and we're going to have a chance to see what it means to follow him as God's** (point up) **chosen King and Son.**

BREATHTAKING BAY: TALK IDEA 2

Suitable for a mid-week club or children's Christianity Explored ***course, ages 8-11***

You will need:

- A bandage or sling
- The *Epic Logbook*
- The Explorer Notebook (see page 156)
- The following visual aids ready to display as you go through the talk

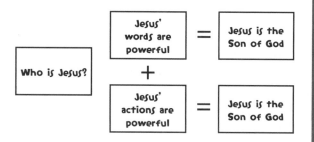

This talk outline can also be downloaded from www.ceministries.org/epic

---

I wonder, who do you think Jesus is?

Display the question: "Who is Jesus?"
You could use a flip chart or PowerPoint.

Maybe you think he was a really cool magician or a clever teacher. Maybe you imagine him to have been a kind man or a genie granting wishes. Or maybe you just think he's made up and never existed.

Lots of people have different ideas about Jesus, so it's important that we explore for ourselves, by examining the evidence of his life and death.

And to do that, we are going to look at Mark's book in the Bible. Mark spent lots of time with people who knew Jesus, and he wrote his discoveries down, because he wanted us to be able to answer the question: Who is Jesus? Mark begins straight away with the answer: Jesus is God's chosen King and Son.

- Read aloud Mark 1:1

Note: Read from the same Bible version you are using with the children. Epic Explorers *uses the 2011 edition of the*

New International Version (NIV), but you may want to adapt the talk to whatever version the children will be using in their discussion groups.

Mark spends the rest of his book explaining why he believes this is true, and why it's good news that Jesus came. So let's explore some of the things Jesus said and did, and see what they show about Jesus.

1. Jesus' words are powerful because he is the Son of God

- Read aloud Mark 1:16-20, asking the children to listen carefully for anything Jesus did that was amazing.

Did you spot what amazing thing Jesus did? (Take responses.)

Jesus gave a command and immediately, Simon, Andrew, James and John obeyed. Just like that (click fingers or do something similar). **There was no ignoring or delaying. No excuses or "Do I have to?". It wasn't like when your mum asks you to tidy your room.**

Nope. They were willing to do what Jesus asked right away. Even though that meant leaving their families and their jobs.

Imagine if I came up to you and said: "Hey, I want you to leave school, forget your family and let me take you wherever I choose". Would you do it? Of course not; not really. I'm not important.

So why did these four leave everything for Jesus? Well, they could tell he was powerful and important from what they had seen and heard about him, and from him. If Jesus said: "Follow", they knew they had to obey.

As the fishermen followed Jesus, they heard Jesus' powerful words again and again. Listen to verses 21-22:

- Read aloud Mark 1:21-22, again asking the children to listen carefully for anything Jesus did that was amazing.

Did you spot the amazing thing Jesus did this time? (Take responses.)

The fishermen heard Jesus teach about God in an amazing way that no one else taught. Jesus' words are powerful.

In fact, his words were so powerful that he was able to heal a man who had an evil spirit. Just like that (click fingers). When Jesus told the evil spirit to leave the man, the spirit obeyed – it had no choice. Jesus' words are powerful.

Why are his words so powerful? How can he just speak, and the impossible happens – and not just here, but all through Mark's book? Well, it's because Jesus is the Son of God, and God has power over everything. He made everything and rules over everything.

Stick up: "Jesus' words are powerful = Jesus is the Son of God"

2) Jesus' actions are powerful because he is the Son of God

But it's not just Jesus' words that are powerful; his actions are as well. Mark gives even more evidence that Jesus is the Son of God.

Can I have a volunteer for a minute?

Bandage the volunteer's arm, or put it in a sling.

I want you to imagine that _____ (volunteer's name) has broken their arm.

Can I make it better just like that?

Click fingers and encourage the children to respond to the question.

Can a doctor make it better just like that?

Click fingers and again encourage the children to respond to the question.

Of course we can't; we don't have that kind of power – but Jesus does. So in Mark 1, when Jesus went back to Simon's house, where Simon's mother-in-law was ill, guess what he did? (Take responses.)

Yes, that's right, Jesus healed her. Just like that (click fingers).

And then lots of others came to the house; many who were sick, many who had evil spirits in them. Guess what Jesus did this time? (Take responses.)

Yes, Jesus healed them. Just like that (click fingers). No disease was too difficult for Jesus – absolutely nothing was incurable.

We see that in the rest of Mark's book too – time and again Jesus made blind people see, deaf people hear and lame people walk. He cleaned up people's skin, he stopped people's bleeding – he even brought people back from the dead.

Jesus' actions are powerful; he can do the impossible, because he made everything and rules over everything. Jesus is the Son of God.

Stick up: "Jesus' actions are powerful = Jesus is the Son of God"

As we discover more about Jesus, we'll keep a record of those discoveries in this Explorer Notebook.

Show page 1 of the Explorer Notebook: "Jesus is God's Son…"

So as we've explored Mark chapter 1, we've seen that Jesus can say and do things that only God has the power to do. This is why Mark believes Jesus is God's chosen King and Son.

But what about you? I wonder, who do you think Jesus is?

Hold up the *Epic Logbook* and show page 3: "Jesus is God's Son"

That's what we'll be thinking about when we split into our small groups.

Ideas menu

INTRODUCTORY ACTIVITIES

Choose at least one of the following activities, to suit your group, your context and the time you have available. Most of the games can be adapted to work from the front or in a small-group setting.

"Who am I?" quiz

Aim: To help the children begin to see that the more clues we have, the easier it is to identify someone.

You will need clues for five famous characters (see below – you may need to replace some of these if your group will not know them).

1. Split the children into teams, if they are not already in groups.

2. Read out one clue at a time. A team can guess at any time, but if they get it wrong, they are out until the next round.

3. If a team guesses correctly, award them points:
   – After clue 1 – 10 points
   – After clue 2 – 8 points
   – After clue 3 – 6 points
   – After clue 4 – 4 points
   – After clue 5 – 2 points

4. Repeat with all the characters.

At the end, explain that the more clues you had, the easier it was to work out who the person is. Today we're going to be collecting clues on some of the things Jesus says and does, and it should help us work out who he really is.

Actions speak louder than words

Aim: To help the children begin to see that the more clues we have, the easier it is to identify someone.

You will need the clues (page 61) and pictures (there are plenty to choose from online).

"Who am I?" quiz questions

Dora the Explorer
- I love to go on new quests and adventures.
- On my travels I have to solve riddles.
- Swiper is my foxy enemy.
- I can speak Spanish.
- My monkey friend, Boots, loves to explore with me.

Bart Simpson
- There are five people in my family.
- I love making prank calls.
- I am often in trouble at school and have to write lines.
- One of my sisters plays the saxophone.
- I am yellow.

Mr. Incredible
- My other name is Bob Parr.
- I wear red.
- I am married with three children.
- I am very strong.
- I am a superhero.

Jessie (Toy Story)
- I wear my hair in a plait with a yellow bow.
- I am excitable, brave and athletic.
- I am scared of the dark.
- Buzz Lightyear is one of my friends.
- I am a cowgirl doll.

Scooby Doo
- I am on TV.
- I help to solve mysteries.
- I have a nephew and four good friends.
- I am a Great Dane.
- I howl when I'm scared

Actions speak louder than words – picture clues

Conductor

- He makes music by waving a stick.
- He can make loud noises by the nod of his head or the shake of his wrist.
- He can make an orchestra sound incredible.

Doctor

- She often works long hours, looking after people.
- She sometimes performs operations.
- She can help you when you are ill.

Firefighter

- They operate hoses and other equipment.
- They have to be lift heavy things and climb ladders.
- They can put out fires.

Lollipop lady / crossing guard

- She has to keep an eye on cars.
- She can stop traffic.
- She helps you cross the road.

Caretaker

- He often works early in the morning.
- He keeps things tidy.
- He fixes things.

1. Beforehand, stick up pictures around the walls.

2. Explain that often we can tell who someone is by what they do.

3. Read out the clues and ask them to run to the picture they think matches the clues.

4. With a larger group, you could split them into teams and just have a runner going for each team. Award a point for the first person there.

Afterwards, explain that these people's actions helped us see who they were. Today we're going to look at some of Jesus' actions to see who he is – God's Son.

All about me

Aims: To help the children begin to see that the more clues we have, the easier it is to identify someone; to get to know the others in the group.

1. Give the children their booklets (*Logbook* for 8-11s or *Scratch Pad* for 4-7s). Ask them to complete "All about me" on page 4.

2. Collect the booklets and read out some of the answers. The other children have to guess whose book it is.

At the end, explain that when we gather information about a person, it helps us understand who they are. Today we're going to be gathering information about Jesus and working out who he is.

Do this, do that

Aim: To introduce the idea that we listen to and obey people who are in charge.

1. Explain to the children that every time you say: "Do this", they must copy the action you're doing. However, if you say: "Do that", they must ignore you.

2. Say: "Do this", then swing your arms. Check the children are copying.

3. Say: "Do that", then stomp your feet. Hopefully no one will copy.

4. Start the game with no one going out, but after a few turns, begin to eliminate the children and pick up the pace.

5. Give points / a prize to the winner(s).

At the end, explain that they listened really well and showed who was in charge by obeying what you said. We're going to see today how Jesus' "words in action" showed he was in charge.

MEMORY VERSE

The memory verse for the week is Mark 10:45.

> *"For even the Son of Man did not come to be served, but to serve, and to give his life as a ransom for many."*

It's important that the verse is explained clearly and concisely, whether you teach a different section each day or teach the whole verse immediately.

Explanations could include:

- **"The Son of Man"** is another special name for God's King and Son. Jesus calls himself "the Son of Man" because he wants us to know that he is fully human, as well as fully God. But he also calls himself "the Son of Man" because hundreds of years earlier, God had promised he would send "the Son of Man", who would be a fantastic King, ruling over everything. Jesus is that King; he is God with us – and he wanted people to know that.

- **"Did not come to be served, but to serve."** If someone is very rich or powerful or important, they usually have servants working for them, people they can boss around. But Jesus tells us here that, even though he's God's Son and a mighty King, he didn't come to be waited on. He didn't come so that people would do something for him. He came to do something for people. Jesus came to serve, to help, to save. Isn't that incredible?! Jesus, the all-powerful one, chose to make himself like a servant – and the most amazing way he did this was to die on the cross to pay for the wrong things we have done.

   A quick sketch could illustrate this with a king calling for their servant, who runs in carrying a glass of water and bows. The king then stands up from their throne, asks the servant to sit down, passes them the water and a newspaper, and gets them a footrest.

- **"And to give his life as a ransom for many."** If something has been stolen, then a thief will sometimes ask for a price to be paid before they will give the item back to the owner. It's called a ransom, when the price is paid to buy something back. When Jesus died, he took the punishment for the wrong things we do. He paid the price so we can be bought back and belong in God's family. Jesus loves us so much that he gave his life as a ransom, so we can be his forever forgiven friends.

  A quick kidnapping sketch could illustrate this, where someone is bought back after the price is paid in full.

- **"Mark 10 verse 45"** is where this verse is found in the Bible. If someone needs to find where we live, they look at our address to discover our town, our street and house number. If we want to find something in the Bible, we have a similar way of looking it up. We look for the book name, chapter and verse number. "Mark" tells us that this sentence is in the Bible book called Mark; the "10" tells us which chapter, and the "45" tells us which verse of that chapter.

You may want to put the memory verse to music to try and help the children learn it. One version is available on Colin Buchanan's "Boom Chicka Boom" album, track 6.

Repetition, actions and visual cues will all help the children memorize the verse. Here's an idea for how you could teach it in Session 1.

Build up memory verse

For even the Son of Man

You will need:

- A picture of a crown with "For even the Son of Man" written on it
- A picture of a servant with "did not come to be served but to serve" written on it
- A picture of a moneybag with "and to give his life as a ransom for many" written on it
- A picture of a Bible with "Mark 10:45" on it

1. Build up the verse in stages, showing a picture at a time, and explaining each phrase.

2. When you have run through it a few times, remove different pieces, until the children can say the whole verse without any prompts.

THEMED SNACK

Fish

You will need:
- Small pretzels
- Cheese slices
- Raisins
- A small, round biscuit/cookie cutter
- Paper plates

1. Use the biscuit/cookie cutters to cut circles out of the cheese slices.

2. Put the pretzels on the plate.

3. Put a cheese circle on top the pretzel to make the fish body. Some of the pretzel should still be showing as the fish tail.

4. Add the raisin to make an eye for the fish.

5. Chat about how Simon, Andrew, James and John all immediately stopped fishing when Jesus called them.

PRAYER SUGGESTION

If you have non-church children at *Epic Explorers*, they may have little or no understanding of prayer. Explain that praying simply means talking to God. We can talk to him anywhere, at anytime and about anything.

When people pray together, they often end by saying "Amen". This means "I agree" and is a way of joining in with the prayer. It's like saying: "Yes, I agree, I want to pray that too". Let the children know that if they don't want to join in, that's fine – they can sit quietly and listen.

Pray a short, simple prayer thanking God for sending his Son, Jesus. Encourage the children to join in at the end if they want to by saying "Amen".

CRAFT IDEAS

4-7s: Paper-plate fish

You will need:
- Paper plates
- Scissors
- Staplers
- Felt-tip pens
- Finger-paint pads
- Wet wipes

1. Cut a wedge from the paper plate. The gap will be the fish mouth.

2. Staple the wedge to the other side of the plate as the tail.

3. Draw an eye above the mouth.

4. Ask the children to draw in the centre of the fish one way they heard about Jesus' power at work.

5. Fingerpaint the edge of the fish.

4-11s: Crowns

You will need:
- Cardboard tubes
- Scissors
- Glue
- Tissue paper
- Jewelled stickers

1. Cut mini crowns out of cardboard tubes in advance.

2. Children to decorate by tearing up tissue paper and gluing on. Cover the crown.

3. Add jewels.

4-11s: Big-surprise puppets

You will need:
- Paper bags
- Cup-cake cases
- Balloons
- Felt-tip pens
- Wool or shredded paper

- Glue
- Red pipe cleaners
- Sticky tape

1. Give the children a paper bag each and ask them to glue on two cup-cake cases as eyes.

2. They can then draw a smaller circle inside the big eyes to try and give their face a "surprised" look.

3. Have each child partly blow up a balloon. They will probably need you to tie it. Stick it onto the paper bag with sticky tape as the nose.

4. Then ask the children to take their pipe cleaner and make it into a surprised mouth shape. Stick onto the bag using sticky tape.

5. Add "hair" to the top of the bag by gluing on wool or shredded paper.

6. On the back of bag, ask the children to write: "People were amazed at Jesus' power".

8-11s: Follow-me fish

You will need:
- Some air-drying clay
- Wooden skewers
- Necklace cord

1. Give each child some clay; then ask them to create a fish shape as a pendant.

2. Encourage them to carve the words "Follow me" on their fish, using the skewer.

3. Using the skewer, make a hole in the fish to thread the cord through.

4. Distribute cord for the pendants.

TEAM CHALLENGE

Team challenges create team spirit and an enthusiastic environment. If you have divided the children into teams, get a representative from each one. Encourage the crowd to spur the players on. You could do several challenges a day (there are extra challenges available to download from www.ceministries.org/epic).

Let's go fishing!

You will need:
- Small ring donuts
- Garden canes x 2
- String
- Chocolate sauce in a bowl
- Chairs
- Aprons or shirts to protect clothes

1. Beforehand, make two fishing rods by tying the string to the cane. Tie a donut to the end of the string.

2. Have two children up from each team. One is to put on an apron/shirt, sit on the chair and be willing to eat the donut.

3. The other child from each team is given the fishing rod. They have to dunk it in the chocolate and then dangle it over the head of the seated child.

4. The seated child has to eat the donut without using their hands. The first to do so wins.

DRAMA

In today's drama, the five Epic Explorers arrive at Breathtaking Bay. Crop discovers the message in a bottle, but Beak's sandwich is stolen by a bird and he refuses to explore any more of the island. See page 148.

EPIC SCRATCH PAD
DISCUSSION GROUPS FOR 4-7s

Bible passage: Mark 1:1, 16-34

Main aims

- Children will know that Jesus has authority over everything.
- Children will understand that Jesus is God's Son.

Introduction

- Start by introducing yourself and asking the children their names.

- If this is part of a holiday club or vacation Bible school, you may also want to ask them what they have liked best so far… and maybe share with them your favourite bit too!

- Explain how this part of the session will work, eg: "We're going to be talking together about the bit of the Bible we've just looked at. We will work through some questions, but it would be great if you ask your own questions too, as we explore. And it's absolutely fine to say: 'I don't get it' or 'Why?' or 'I don't think I agree'."

- Explain that no one will be asked to read out loud, pray or answer a question if they don't want to.

Scratch Pad

If there's time and it's one of your chosen introductory activities, turn to page 4 of the *Scratch Pad* and complete "All about me"*. (See page 61 of this Leader's Guide for how to run this activity.)

For the first question, ask the children to circle the shade they prefer. The instruction simply says: "I like this one best". We phrased it this way so that children wouldn't get confused by the "wrong" spelling of favourite/favorite and colour/color!

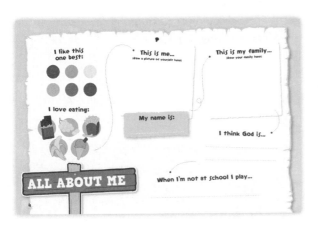

Photo findings

The recap below (called "Photo findings") appears on page 5 of the *Epic Scratch Pad*. It is a simple storyboard with the teaching summarized.

- Jesus' words have power.
- Jesus is God's Son. He is King of everything.
- Jesus' power amazes!

As you look at the pictures, if you have time, you could ask the children to tell you if they remember what is happening.

Questions

Use the questions on pages 5 and 6 to encourage discussion.

1. Draw what Simon and Andrew used to catch.

Question 1 is pretty straightforward as the children just need to draw fish. Don't forget to sell it to them, eg: "Who here is clever enough to remember from the story?"

2. All the men stopped what they were doing to follow who?

The options are: a police officer, a king, or Jesus, God's Son.

Afterwards explain that they listened to and obeyed Jesus because he is in charge. He is more important than a police officer and more powerful than a king. He is in charge of the whole world because he is God! That's why the fishermen were willing to leave their jobs and their families immediately.

3. Jesus showed lots of power in the way he spoke and acted. He taught and helped lots of people. How did they feel?

The people were amazed as Jesus showed his authority and power in the story, eg: in commanding the evil spirit, in healing the people who were ill, and in his teaching.

Write in the blanks that Jesus' power shows us that he is **God**.

After they've written their answer, ask if the children know any other ways that Jesus showed his authority and power. For example, he fed 5000, stopped a storm, etc.

4. Do you think Jesus is just as powerful today? Why?

Most children will just be able to write "yes" or "no", but use further questions to see if they are able to explain why. They may say they don't know. As the sessions go on, they may change their opinions and go back to change their answers. You may want to share with them one reason why you believe Jesus is still just as powerful.

5. How do you think Jesus can help you? Draw your answer...

There is nothing wrong if the children draw Jesus making them better etc., but why not ask further questions to discover if your group understand anything of the gospel message? Eg:

- *Does anyone know how Jesus can rescue us?* We're going to be thinking about that in the next few sessions; or

- *Does anyone know how we can be God's friends?* We're going to discover how in the next few sessions.

If you have time, you may want to let the children do the puzzles on page 7, with some informal chat. If this is part of a holiday club or vacation Bible school, then the puzzle time is also a good opportunity to practise the memory verse and to plug any upcoming events or regular clubs.

Conclusion

Finish by encouraging your group members to come back next time. Tell them: "We've seen some of the incredible things Jesus said and did. Next time we're going to explore why he came."

Evaluate

- Jot down the name of each child in your group on a separate note card. Add anything you remember about their interests, as well as their level of understanding. Use the cards as prompts to pray for the children between sessions. You can add to them as the course goes on.

- Consider the different personalities in the group and if you need to change the way in which you facilitate discussion to draw everyone in.

- Pray that God will unveil their eyes so they will see who Jesus is.

(A downloadable version of these leader's notes for discussion groups is available from www.ceministries.org/epic.)

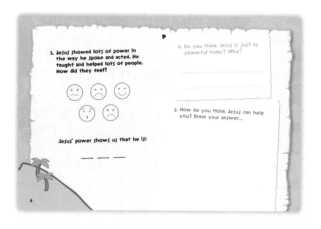

EPIC LOGBOOK
DISCUSSION GROUPS FOR 8-11s

Bible passage: Mark 1:1, 16-34

Main aims

- Children will know that Jesus has authority over everything.
- Children will understand that Jesus is God's Son.

Introduction

- Start by introducing yourself and asking the children their names.

- If this is part of a holiday club or vacation Bible school, you may also want to ask them what they have liked best so far… and maybe share with them your favourite bit too!

- Explain how this part of the session will work, eg: "We're going to be talking together about the bit of the Bible we've just looked at. We will work through some questions, but it would be great if you ask your own questions too, as we explore. And it's absolutely fine to say: 'I don't get it' or 'Why?' or 'I don't think I agree'."

- Explain that no one will be asked to read out loud, pray or answer a question if they don't want to.

Booklet

If there's time and it's one of your chosen introductory activities, turn to page 4 of the *Logbook* and complete "All about me". (See page 61 of this Leader's Guide for how to run this activity.)

Explorer's entries

The recap below (called "Explorer's entries") appears on page 5 of the *Epic Logbook*. If you have time, you may want to read through and summarize.

- Mark 1:1 – Jesus is God's Son. He is King of everything.
- Mark 1:16-20 – Jesus has power in his words.
- Mark 1:21-28 – Jesus has power over evil.
- Mark 1:29-34 – Jesus has power over sickness.

Questions

Use the questions on pages 5 and 6 to encourage discussion.

1. **What did Simon, Andrew, James and John do, and why was it surprising? (See Mark 1:18 and 20.)**

The children are likely to answer easily that the men stopped fishing, left everything and followed Jesus. They may struggle initially to identify the surprise, so you may want to ask the group how they think *they* would have responded in the same situation. It is surprising because the men didn't protest or try to delay. Rather, they were willing to leave their jobs, families and security immediately.

2. **How else did Jesus show he was more than an ordinary man?**

Help the children think how Jesus showed his authority and power in the story, eg: in commanding the evil spirit, in healing the people who were

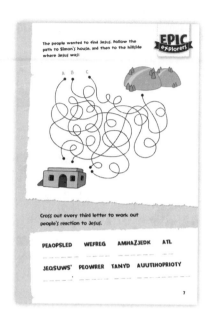

If you have time, you may want to let the children do the puzzles on page 7, with some informal chat. If this is part of a holiday club or vacation Bible school, then the puzzle time is also a good opportunity to practise the memory verse and to plug any upcoming events or regular clubs.

ill, and in his teaching straight from God. After they've written their answers, ask if the children know any other ways that Jesus showed his authority and power? For example, he fed 5000, stopped a storm, etc.

3. Which of these events in Mark 1 do you find the most amazing? Why?

This question is to encourage the children to think more deeply about the miracles described in Mark 1. Help them to understand that Jesus wasn't performing tricks, but rather, doing things that only God can do. Jesus' miracles are signposts to who he is. Be prepared to answer questions on evil spirits if anyone asks.

4. Do you think Jesus has just as much power and authority today? Why?

Use this question as an opportunity to check your group's spiritual temperature and understanding. They may well answer that they don't know. As the weeks go on, they may change their opinions and go back to change their answers. You may want to share with them one reason why you believe Jesus is still just as powerful.

5. What do you think these events have to do with us?

The children may say "nothing at all" but point out that God wants most of all for us to love him and follow him. The children may be amazed at Jesus' power, intrigued to find out more, or wanting to obey him by doing what he says, even if that means stopping doing something else.

Conclusion

Finish by encouraging your group members to come back next time. Tell them: "We've seen some of the incredible things Jesus said and did. Next time we're going to explore why he came."

Evaluate

- Jot down the name of each child in your group on a separate note card. Add anything you remember about their interests, as well as their level of understanding. Use the cards as prompts to pray for the children between sessions. You can add to them as the course goes on.

- Consider the different personalities in the group and if you need to change the way in which you facilitate discussion to draw everyone in.

- Pray that God will unveil their eyes so they will see who Jesus is.

(A downloadable version of these leader's notes for discussion groups is available from www.ceministries.org/epic.)

DISCOVERY DENS
Jesus forgives sins

Bible passage
Mark 2:1-17

Main aims
- Children will know that we don't treat God as we should and that our biggest problem is our sin.
- Children will understand that only Jesus has power to forgive sin and can rescue us.

Session options
The following pages include a wide variety of activities. See pages 14-19 for suggestions of which activities to choose for different contexts or length of time.

Notes for leaders
Read Mark 2:1-17

All through Mark's Gospel, we see the *identity* and *mission* of Jesus addressed: who he is and why he came. The miracle in 2:1-12 and the call of Levi in 2:13-17 bring these two themes together. We see Jesus' unique authority over nature and illness clearly revealed – and all that his power can achieve, namely the forgiveness of sin.

The account in verses 1-12 is a familiar one to many of us, so it's important we don't miss the surprise that would have been experienced at the original incident. There Jesus is preaching (verse 2), when four highly-motivated men decide to interrupt the proceedings by ripping up the roof in order to deliver their paralytic friend to the feet of Jesus, (verses 3-4). What commitment and faith they show!

The surprise comes in verse 5 as Jesus, rather than immediately healing the paralytic physically (which is what he and his friends were no doubt expecting), tells the man that he's forgiven, due to the faith shown in Jesus. Clearly, forgiveness of sin and dealing with sinners is the top priority – the urgent need in Jesus' eyes. While healing brings pain relief this side of eternity, it does not deal with our sin problem, which has eternal repercussions (Romans 6:23).

Jesus, as God's only Son and King (Mark 1:1), is the only one able to offer forgiveness for the way we treat God. He is the only one who can pardon us and save us from the punishment we deserve.

Leader's checklist
Have you...

- ☐ Invited the children, and made clear the time and place where you will meet?
- ☐ Collected parental consent forms for any new children?
- ☐ Assigned leaders to the various activities and discussion groups?
- ☐ Prepared the talk, including any visual aids?
- ☐ Collected any items needed for the activities?
- ☐ *Epic Scratch Pads* (4-7s) and/or *Epic Logbooks* (8-11s) and a pencil for each child?
- ☐ Prepared the activities and questions for the discussion groups?
- ☐ Enough Bibles or Mark's Gospels for everyone, if you are using them?
- ☐ (Optional) Rehearsed the drama and collected props?
- ☐ Prayed for each group member and yourself as the leader?

It's at this point we meet, for the first time in Mark's Gospel, the opposition of the Jewish leaders. Their objection in verse 7 is linked to their belief that only God can forgive sin, since sin is an offence against God. While they are right in their belief, they are wrong in their failure to acknowledge that Jesus therefore is God – even when he gives evidence for his divinity in:

- knowing what they are thinking (verse 8)
- calling himself the Son of Man (verse 10, and see Daniel 7:13-15)
- making the man walk (verses 11-12; Isaiah 35:6).

Jesus' work is invisible, but he proves it by healing the man physically and visibly. The result is amazement once again (verse 12), despite the leaders' hostility.

While it's easy to mock the Pharisees, we all too easily fall into the same trap. We rarely see forgiveness as our greatest need, failing to address the sin in our hearts, and concentrating instead on more comfortable topics and the things that are around us. When we think about what we need, it's all too easy to focus on our immediate needs, rather than lie at our Saviour's feet and plead for his mercy.

In verses 14-17, we see Jesus calling another disciple, but Levi is no ordinary man – he's a tax collector! Tax collectors were social and spiritual outcasts. They worked for the ruling Romans and cheated their own countrymen, so they were seen as the enemies of God and his people.

What was deeply shocking at the time was the fact that Jesus not only called Levi to follow him, but he then went on to eat with Levi and a number of his undesirable friends (verse 15). The teachers of the law were once again unimpressed (verse 16), as Jesus' actions implied he had shown mercy and accepted Levi and the other outcasts, rather than adhering to the rules and regulations of the religious leaders.

If Jesus' top priority is forgiving sin, then here the sin doctor is in full swing as he responds to the criticism (verse 17). Jesus tells us why he has come – he has come to save sinners. The big question that should raise is how (answered in session 3 on the cross!).

Leader's prayer: Let's pray that we will be those who see our own sin and who help others see their sin. Let's pray that as they do so, they will humbly confess their sin and joyfully accept Jesus' offer of mercy. May they be like the crowd who praised God (verse 12).

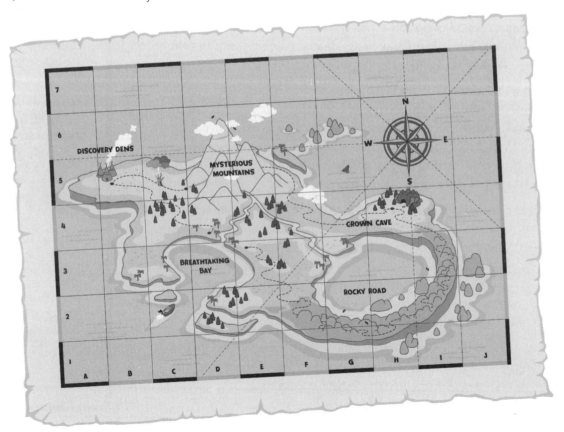

DISCOVERY DENS: TALK IDEA 1

Suitable for a holiday club or vacation Bible school, ages 4-11 or 8-11

You will need:
- Simple costume for each character being interviewed*:
  - Eyewitness – Sunglasses and wig
  - Paralyzed man – A bed roll and hat
  - Levi – Baseball cap and money bag
  - Professor – White lab coat
- The Island map visual with the "Breathtaking Bay" coloured visual attached (see pages 152-154)
- The "Discovery Dens" coloured visual

* *If you only have two actors, one could play the eyewitness and Levi, with a very quick costume change, and the other could play the paralyzed man and professor. It is also possible for one actor to play all four parts.*

This talk outline can also be downloaded from www.ceministries.org/epic

Reporter: Welcome to Capernaum News. It seems that Jesus of Nazareth has been doing more amazing things. Earlier we reported on the events at Breathtaking Bay (point to the map). Once again Jesus has been healing people and speaking with God's authority.

We're going to be talking to some men who were in the Discovery Dens (point to the map), and we'll be asking the question: what really matters to Jesus? So without further ado, let me introduce you to our first guest.

On walks the first eyewitness.

Reporter: Good evening and thanks for being here. I wonder – can you fill us in on the day's happenings?

Eyewitness: Yes of course. It all began when I heard that Jesus was back in Capernaum. I was desperate to see him in action and so I went to the house he was visiting, as did every man and his dog, it seemed. We all packed in, watching and listening.

Then, above us, there was loads of banging and bits of the roof started crumbling. I looked up – and I saw four guys peering through a hole in the roof!

Reporter: You're joking? People were so keen to see Jesus that they destroyed a roof? Why?

Eyewitness: Well, it seemed they had brought their paralyzed friend to see Jesus, but couldn't get to him because of the crowds. However, they were so convinced that Jesus would heal their friend, they wouldn't give up. They had this genius idea to lower him on his mat through the roof and land him in front of Jesus!

Reporter: Amazing! What faith these guys had in Jesus' power! So what happened next? Did Jesus heal him immediately?

Eyewitness: Not quite. Jesus turned to him and said: "Your sins are forgiven".

Reporter: He said what?

Eyewitness: "Your sins are forgiven!"

Reporter: He never! The man was paralyzed – that's why his friends had taken him – so Jesus could heal him! Does Jesus think that the forgiveness of sin matters more than walking?

Eyewitness: Yes, he must do – and the religious leaders weren't happy about that, let me tell you. They didn't think Jesus was able to forgive sins because they know that only God can forgive sins. But what the leaders didn't realise is – Jesus IS God.

Reporter: Wow! To find out what happened next, we've invited the paralyzed man himself to come into the studio.

In walks the paralyzed man.

Reporter: Great to have you here. Now, obviously you've just walked in, so can you tell us what happened after Jesus said he'd forgiven you?

Paralyzed man: Well, he proved that he IS God. First, by pointing out what the leaders were thinking; and then he told me to get up with my mat and walk home. And that's exactly what I did. Everyone was flabbergasted!

Reporter: Incredible. So Jesus proved that he is God, both in his actions and in his words; and he showed that the forgiveness of sins really matters.

We've more evidence of this from another incident today. And so I've asked Levi the tax collector to come and share that evidence. Levi, welcome.

Levi walks in. Give him a strong regional accent to add some fun to his account.

Reporter: Levi, please tell us about your meeting with Jesus.

Levi: Sure. Well, there I was, collecting in everyone's money to pass on to the Romans, when up walks Jesus. Now, I don't mind telling you – I was a little bit surprised. No one likes hanging round with guys like me. We're the lowest of the low, you know, cheats'n'all.

But anyway, he comes up to me and tells me to follow him. Spoke with such authority, I had to. And then, I invited him back to my place to have a meal with some of my friends. Well, that didn't sit right with the religious leaders. They were really cross that Jesus was hanging out with us.

Reporter: I'm sure they weren't impressed. So, what did Jesus say?

Levi: Well, to sum it up, he basically said that he'd come to save sinners. That's it in a nutshell. Amazing!

Reporter: So again we see that the forgiveness of sin really matters to Jesus. To help us understand why it's such a big deal, we've invited an expert on this issue of sin.

Professor enters.

Reporter: Professor, why do you think sin matters so much to Jesus?

Professor: It's like this: we all sin – all of us do things wrong, say things wrong and think things wrong – and as a result we are cut off from God. And the only way for us to be friends with God again is to be forgiven by him.

It appears that Jesus came to earth to make a way for us to be forgiven and saved from the punishment we deserve.

Reporter: Well, that really is good news. We've discovered our forgiveness is what really matters, because otherwise we're separated from God. And Jesus has come to make our forgiveness possible.

Stick up "Discovery Dens" visual with an amazed face.

Reporter: Amazing! That's all from us here at Capernaum on this historic day. Join us again tomorrow for the latest on Jesus, the Son of God. But for now, good night.

DISCOVERY DENS: TALK IDEA 2

Suitable for a mid-week club or children's Christianity Explored course, ages 8-11

You will need:

- 6 large story picture cards (or these can be on PowerPoint if you're teaching a big group) – available to download from www.ceministries.org/epic
- Visuals from session 1, already displayed as a reminder of what we learned last time
- The Explorer Notebook (see page 156)
- Depending on illustration choice, either a "Shove off God, I'm in charge, Not you" visual or a Treasure Island map with a treasure chest on it, an "X" to stick on, a blindfold and the phrase "Sin is missing God's mark"
- 3 arrows and 3 slips of paper with "It spoils", "It separates" and "We're stuck" written on them

This talk outline can also be downloaded from www.ceministries.org/epic

What do you think your biggest problem is? Is it the fact you have to sit next to the class bully? Or that you haven't been picked for the school team? Maybe it's something to do with your family or friends. Well, in chapter 2 of Mark's Gospel, we see that Jesus thinks we have a bigger problem. A problem that *spoils* and *separates*. A problem that gets us *stuck*.

Let's go back to Capernaum:

Show picture 1: A house where you can see people through the doorway and window, and surrounding the outside of the house.

There you are, rammed in the crowded house and I mean rammed! People are squashed into every nook and cranny, packed into every space possible, inside the house and outside. You see, Jesus is there and everyone is desperate to hear him speaking. You all know that his words are powerful.

Point to the "Jesus' words are powerful" visual from session 1.

Show picture 2: Inside the house, with a hole in the roof and the paralyzed man being lowered down.

All of a sudden, bits of the roof start bouncing off your head. You look up and see a gaping hole, with four men lowering their friend down on his mat. They have brought him to Jesus to be healed. They believe that Jesus can help because they know his actions are powerful.

Point to the "Jesus' actions are powerful" visual from session 1.

As the man lands right in front of Jesus, the friends are watching, you're watching, the man's waiting... What would you expect to happen next? (Take answers.)

But listen to what actually happened:

- Read aloud Mark 2:5

Show picture 3: Inside the house, the crowd with shocked faces and a speech bubble saying: "Your sins are forgiven".

Jesus doesn't heal the man right away – he doesn't do what everyone's expecting – instead Jesus forgives the man's sins. But why? We need to make sure we understand what sin is to see why.

So what is sin?

Note: Use one of the two illustrations below to explain what sin is. The first one is especially useful for church children as it is more relational and will help them see that sin is not merely about actions.

Illustration 1:
Sin is when we don't treat God as we should. It's like we're saying: "Shove off God. I'm in charge, Not you!".

Stick up: **S**hove off God
I'm in charge
Not you!

Sin isn't just the wrong things we say or do, but it's also to do with our attitude towards God. Sin is when we make ourselves...

Point to the "I" in the visual aid.

... more important than God, even though he is in charge and wants the best for us.

So when you disobey God's commands and do what *you* want instead, such as lying to someone or taking something that doesn't belong to you, it's as if you are saying: "Shove off God – your rules are wrong, I'm in charge, not you!"

And when you forget about God, or love things like sport or TV or friends more than God, it's as if you are saying: "Shove off God – you don't matter, I'm in charge, not you!"

The Bible says that all of us sin and that there are serious consequences for our sin.

Illustration 2:
Sin basically means missing God's mark.

Stick up "Sin is missing God's mark" and then ask for a volunteer to stick an "X" on your treasure map, where the treasure chest is. But blindfold them before they try. Comment on whether or not they meet the mark by putting the "X" in the correct place.

You see, God has set a mark for us. It's to "love the Lord your God with all your heart" and "love your neighbour as you love your-self". But none of us manage to do this all the time, so none of us manage to meet God's mark.

Sometimes we miss his mark by not bother-ing to speak to him or considering him in our decisions. Or sometimes we disobey his instructions – like the time you lied to your mum. All of us say, think and do things that are wrong. All of us ignore God. This is a lot more serious than missing the treasure in the game, as it has serious consequences...

Note: Whichever illustration you have used, the talk continues from this point.

What are the consequences of sin?

Stick up an arrow going from your definition of sin, as explained in your chosen illustration, and then add "It spoils". Build the visual aid up each time so that it looks like this:

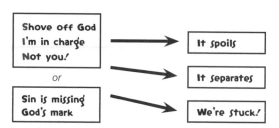

1. It spoils

Imagine you're playing inside with a tennis racket, despite being told not to. As you sweep your arm back to hit the ball, you hit your TV instead and smash the screen to pieces. What would happen next? (Take one or two answers.)

I imagine you would be sent to your room or punished in another way as you've spoilt things – the TV *and* your family relationships. In fact, any time we sin, it spoils something. If we foul in soccer, we spoil the game. If we lie, we can spoil people's trust in us.

But the most serious consequence of sin is that it spoils our relationship with God and deserves punishment.

Stick up another arrow going from the definition of sin; then add: "It separates".

2. It separates

You see, God is angry with us when we don't live in a way that pleases him. It wouldn't be fair if God just said: "It doesn't matter" when we do something unkind or we don't treat him as we should. And so, we deserve to be punished.

God's punishment is a bit like when we're sent to our room after smashing the TV; then we are separated from our family, but God's punishment is much more serious, as it's sepa-ration from him and his perfect kingdom for ever. In fact, the Bible's name for this eternal separation from God is hell. That's why sin is such a serious problem.

> Stick up an arrow going from the
> definition on sin; then add "We're stuck".

3. We're stuck!

The third problem is that we can't get rid of our sin ourselves – we're stuck.

Some people think that we can fix our sin problem ourselves by making sure we don't do anything unkind or selfish, or by going to church and doing loads of good stuff instead. They think we can make ourselves okay with God.

But that's just like sticking black paper over your TV to try and cover up the damage. We maybe able to hide the smashed screen, but it doesn't deal with the real problem – the TV is still broken.

In the same way, doing good stuff doesn't deal with our biggest problem – our sin still spoils, and it still separates us from God. Which is why we need someone to help us. So is Jesus that person? Let's go back to Mark 2 and find out.

> Show picture 4: Inside the house, the
> Pharisees looking very unhappy, with a
> thought bubble coming from their heads:
> "Only God can forgive sins".

As you look around after Jesus' shocking statement, you see the religious leaders scowling furiously. They think only God can forgive sins, and do you know what? They're right!

> Show picture 5: Inside the house, with
> a speech bubble saying: "Which is
> easier for people to see? If he has been
> forgiven, or he has been healed?"

Jesus knows exactly what they are thinking because he's God's Son.

> Point to the "Jesus is the Son of God"
> visual from session 1.

So Jesus asks them if it's easier to say: "Your sins are forgiven" or to say: "Get up and walk". The answer has to be "Your sins are forgiven" because you can just say it and no one will know if it's true or not. There's no way of actually seeing if someone's sins have been forgiven.

But if you say: "Get up and walk" to a paralyzed man, then of course you can see if they're healed – if it's true, they'll start walking around.

> Show picture 6: Inside the house, with
> the paralytic man standing up and
> everyone looking amazed.

The next thing you know, Jesus proves that he has authority over sin and over sickness by telling the man to get up and go home... and he does. How incredible is that?! Jesus speaks and the man is forgiven; Jesus acts and the man is healed.

Jesus' words are powerful (point to the "Jesus' words are powerful" visual from session 1).

Jesus' actions are powerful (point to the "Jesus' actions are powerful" visual from session 1).

Can you imagine how amazed you would be to see this?

And the great news is, Jesus didn't just come to forgive the man's sin but ours too (show page 2 of the Explorer Notebook).

He is able to do so because he is God's Son (show page 1 of the Explorer Notebook).

Next time we'll see exactly how Jesus deals with the way our sin *spoils* and *separates*. We'll see the rescue he offers so we don't have to be *stuck*.

Ideas menu

INTRODUCTORY ACTIVITIES

Choose at least one of the following activities, to suit your group, your context and the time you have available. Most of the games can be adapted to work from the front or in a small-group setting.

Target games

Aim: To understand that sin is missing God's standards.

You will need various target games, eg: hoopla, balls into a bucket, tin can alley.

1. Split the children into teams.

2. Choose different volunteers from each team to have a go at the different target games.

3. Give points to those who hit the target / do the best.

4. You could do this as a challenge up the front.

Afterwards, talk about how in life all of us fail to reach God's standards. We miss the mark in our words, thoughts and actions. We don't treat God as we should, but today we'll hear that Jesus is able to forgive us.

Picture quiz

Aim: To understand that Jesus can see everything and knows that our biggest need is forgiveness.

You will need cropped pictures of objects, either photocopied or as PowerPoints slides.

1. Show the children the pictures.

2. They have to guess what the objects are.

3. Reveal the answers to them.

Explain that today we'll see a man who appears to have a problem with his legs, but that's only part of the picture. Jesus knew the whole picture – he knew what the man's biggest problem was and what he really needed.

Who has the power?

Aim: To understand that only Jesus has the power to forgive sins.

1. Give the children their *Epic Scratch Pads* or *Logbooks*, and ask them to complete: "Who has the power?" on page 10, eg: "Who has the power to send off a player in football?" (a referee). In the *Scratch Pads*, the children just need to link the matching pictures.

Afterwards, explain that today we will see that Jesus is the only person who has the power to forgive the wrong things we say, think and do.

Blanket relay

Aim: To introduce the story of four men helping their paralyzed friend.

You will need a blanket for each team.

1. Divide the children into teams of five.

2. Have each team stand at the starting line.

3. The teams have to use the blanket to carry one team member to the finish line.

4. Once they reach the end, they swap who is being carried.

5. Repeat until everyone in the team has been carried.

Afterwards, explain that today we are going to hear about four men carrying their friend who couldn't walk to Jesus.

MEMORY VERSE

Marching

The memory verse for the week is Mark 10:45.

"For even the Son of Man did not come to be served, but to serve, and to give his life as a ransom for many."

It's important that the verse is explained clearly and concisely, whether you teach a different section each day or teach the whole verse immediately (see page 62).

1. Have the children marching on the spot. Act like an army general and give them commands, eg: "Touch your toes", "Wave your hand", "Attention!"

2. After a few orders, explain that you're in control and have power over them. That means when you speak, they should obey.

3. Tell the children to keep marching and to obey you by repeating what you say. Call out sections of the verse, in the style of an army chant:

Leader: A one and two and three and four

Children: A one and two and three and four

Leader: This is taken from God's Word

Children: This is taken from God's Word

Leader: For even the Son of Man

Children: For even the Son of Man

Leader: Did not come to be –ee served

Children: Did not come to be –ee served

Leader: Bu-ut to ser-er-erve

Children: Bu-ut to ser-er-erve

Leader: And to give his life as a ransom for many

Children: And to give his life as a ransom for many

Leader: It's found in Mark chapter ten

Children: It's found in Mark chapter ten

Leader: And in verse forty-five

Children: And in verse forty-five

4. Repeat a few times, changing your voice after a couple of goes, eg: whispering, shouting, squeaking, low-pitched, posh, underwater, slow motion, etc. Then remind the children of what the verse is teaching us.

THEMED SNACK

The paralyzed man

You will need:
- Gingerbread men or cookies cut in the shape of a person*
- Icing pens
- Smarties or chocolate buttons
- Strawberry laces
- Small rectangles of card (card stock) for the mat
- Felt-tip pens
- Hole punch

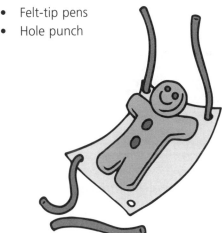

1. Children decorate the gingerbread man or cookie.

2. Colour in the card (card stock) mat and punch a hole in each corner.

3. Give each child two strawberry laces. Snap the strawberry laces in half; then thread each half-lace through a hole and tie.

4. Lay the gingerbread man / cookie on the mat and practice lowering him down. Chat about how Jesus forgave the man first, before healing him, because our biggest problem is our sin.

*Alternatively you could give each child a jelly baby, which they have to lay on a finger biscuit or cracker before eating.

📖 *When you pray with the children, it is good to explain that "amen" means "I agree", and that it gives them the option of joining in.*

You will need:
- A flip chart
- A marker pen

Brainstorm with the children ways that Jesus showed his amazing love and power in today's session and the previous one. Write their suggestions on a flip chart.

Afterwards, ask a leader to pray a prayer of thanksgiving to God for the different ways that Jesus showed he was God's Son, for his kindness and for his power. They should include the children's suggestions from the flip chart.

CRAFT IDEAS

4-7s: Springy legs

You will need:
- Thin strips of paper
- Card (card stock) outlines of a person's head and body (see page 158 or download from www.ceministries.org/epic)
- Sticky tape
- Felt-tip pens

1. Give each child a body outline; then ask them to decorate it.

2. Then give each child two strips of paper and teach them how to fold each strip in a concertina fashion (lots of alternating folds to give a springy effect).

3. Next attach the folded paper as legs to the man's body. They are springy so that the man can jump for joy.

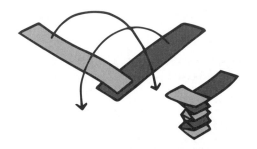

4-11s: Peg doll and mat

You will need:
- Wooden clothes pegs
- Small scraps of fabric, ribbon, lace, felt and wool
- Small buttons
- Googly eyes
- PVA (white) glue
- Glue spreaders
- Felt-tip pens
- Rectangular card for the mat – with "Jesus can forgive sins" written on the mat

1. Spread glue on one side of the peg.

2. Stick pieces of fabric on the peg, leaving a section uncovered for the head.

3. Add extras, eg: ribbon and lace; then glue on eyes and wool for the hair.

4. Then give each child the card to decorate as the mat.

5. The peg person can either lie on the mat or the mat can be rolled up and held by the peg.

4-11s: Mobile

You will need:
- Scissors
- Copies of the lightning bolts and "wow" on card (available to download from www.ceministries.org/epic)
- Single-hole punch
- String or wool
- Felt-tip pens
- Glitter glue

1. Give each child a copy of the lightning bolt and wow template to cut out.

2. Colour in one side of each of the four lightning bolts, and glue on glitter around the edges. Decorate the "wow" also.

3. On the non-coloured side of the lightning bolts, ask the children to write a word on each: "Jesus", "can", "forgive", "sins".

4. Punch holes in each piece and help string the lightning bolts together vertically so they read: "Jesus can forgive sins, wow!"

8-11s: Placemat

You will need:
- Scissors
- Sticky tape
- A4/US letter size paper
- Strips of paper
- Glue
- Optional: laminate pouches and laminator

1. Give each child a sheet of paper. They are to fold the paper in half lengthways, then cut evenly spaced slits starting from the folded edge and continuing up to about 1cm from the opposite edge. It may be helpful to draw lines to use as guides while you cut.

2. Open up the paper and demonstrate to the children how they can weave in an over/under fashion.

3. Take one paper strip and weave it through the slits, going over and under the slits.

4. Push the woven strip to the top and start with a second. It should be woven in an opposite pattern to the first, ie: under then over.

5. Weave more paper strips in an alternating pattern.

6. When finished, get children to secure the ends by taping them to the mat.

7. Next, fold another piece of paper in half and place on the floor. The children are to draw round one foot and then cut out (while the paper is still folded).

8. Stick the two footprints on the mat, using glue.

9. If possible, laminate the mats so they can be used as placemats.

TEAM CHALLENGE

Sensory search

You will need:
- A cardboard box decorated to look like a house
- Dried beans and rice – fill the box with them
- Mystery objects, eg: toy cars, Lego people, marbles, paper clips…

1. Ask for a volunteer from each team to come up and place a hand in the "house".

2. Tell them an item that they need to discover.

3. The first to give you the requested item wins.

DRAMA

In today's drama, the children arrive at Discovery Dens. Berry discovers the next clue, but Rosie falls down a hole and refuses to be helped out. So only Sonny, Crop and Berry continue to explore the island. See page 148.

EPIC SCRATCH PAD
DISCUSSION GROUPS FOR 4-7s

Bible passage: Mark 2:1-17

Main aims

- Children will know that we don't treat God as we should and that our biggest problem is our sin.
- Children will understand that only Jesus has power to forgive sin and can rescue us.

Introduction

- Welcome the children back.

- Learn the names of any new children.

- Remind them of your name.

- Recap on previous session, eg: "Last time, we saw how Jesus showed incredible power in the way he spoke and the things he did. He showed that he is God's only chosen King and Son. But why did he come to earth? That's what we're going to start to think about today."

Booklet

If there's time and it's one of your chosen introductory activities, complete "Who has the power?" on page 10 of the *Scratch Pad*. (See page 76 in this Leader's Guide for how to run this activity.)

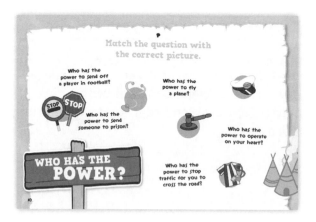

Photo findings

The recap below (called "Photo findings") appears on page 11 of the *Epic Scratch Pad*. It is a simple storyboard with the teaching summarised.

- Jesus came to deal with sin.
- Jesus has the power to forgive.
- Jesus proves he is God's Son.

As you look at the pictures, if you have time, you could ask the children to tell you if they remember what is happening.

Questions

Use the questions on pages 11 and 12 to encourage discussion.

1. **How did the paralyzed man get to Jesus?** (Draw an arrow.) **How many people helped him?**

There's a picture of a house so the children just need to draw an arrow to the roof. Why not get your group to act out carrying their friend up some steps, digging and lowering him down?

After circling how many people helped (4), tell the children it wasn't really important how the lame man got into the house or how many helped. What mattered was the fact that he was taken to Jesus.

2. **How did the people watching feel?**

Ask the children to show you the people's expressions first by acting them out. Then, after they've circled one or more expressions, explain that some people were cross because they didn't understand who Jesus was.

3. We can't do miracles, but Jesus can. He can forgive sins because he is...

Discuss with the children the fact that we can't just make things happen. Maybe have a go at commanding snow to fall or making yourself taller! Remind them that no ordinary person can control everything, so Jesus must be someone special. After the children have filled in the blanks ("God"), ask them to tick their answer to what Jesus has power over:

- ☐ **Everything**
- ☐ **Sickness**
- ☐ **Only big and scary things**
- ☐ **Nothing**

Point out that Jesus is the King of everything and always has been. He made everything and has power over everything. Nothing is bigger or better than Jesus.

4. We sin when we don't treat God as we should. It is a big problem because it separates us from God. Can you draw a wall between the person and God?

After the children have drawn the wall, talk about how our sin is a barrier between us and God. It cuts us off from him. You may want to consider with the children that when they get sent to their room, it's because they have done something wrong and spoilt things with their parents. They are separated from their parents as a punishment. We deserve to be punished for ever by God.

5. Draw something that you have done wrong. Then go over the dots to spell a message about Jesus.

After the children have done a quick drawing and written "Jesus can forgive our sin", explain that

in the next session we will see how Jesus can forgive us. Ask if any of them think they know how Jesus can rescue us and forgive us from the wrong things we do.

If you have time, you may want to let the children do the puzzles on page 13, with some informal chat. If this is part of a holiday club or vacation Bible school, then the puzzle time is also a good opportunity to practise the memory verse and to plug any upcoming events or regular clubs.

Give out invitations to your family event.

Conclusion

Finish by encouraging your group members to come back next time. Tell them: "We've seen what sin is and why it is such a problem, but we've also discovered that Jesus came to deal with our problem. Next time we'll look at how he does that, so make sure you come back to explore the good news!"

Evaluate

- Is there anything you could add to your prayer cards? Was there anyone from the previous session missing today? You may be able to contact them and encourage them to come next time. If not, pray that they will return even without being contacted.

- Do you need to think about how to respond to any particular questions? Make sure you find time to plan your answer.

- Pray that the children will be convicted of their sin and their need of a Saviour.

(A downloadable version of these leader's notes for discussion groups is available from www.ceministries.org/epic.)

EPIC LOGBOOK
DISCUSSION GROUPS FOR 8-11s

Bible passage: Mark 2:1-17

Main aims

- Children will know that we don't treat God as we should and that our biggest problem is our sin.
- Children will understand that only Jesus has power to forgive sin and can rescue us.

Introduction

- Welcome the children back.
- Learn the names of any new children.
- Remind them of your name.
- Recap on previous session, eg: "Last time, we saw how Jesus showed incredible power in the way he spoke and the things he did. He showed that he is God's only chosen King and Son. But why did he come to earth? That's what we're going to start to think about today."

Booklet

If there's time and it's one of your chosen introductory activities, complete "Who has the power?" on page 10 of the *Logbook*. (See page 76 in this Leader's Guide for how to run this activity.)

Explorer's entries

The recap below (called "Explorer's entries") appears on page 11 of the *Epic Logbook*. If you have time, you may want to read through and summarize.

- Mark 2:1-12 – Jesus can forgive sin.
- Mark 2:13-17 – Jesus sees sin as our biggest problem and only he can deal with it.
- Sin is when we don't treat God the way we should. It should be punished.

Questions

Use the questions to encourage discussion.

1. Brainstorm some of the different feelings experienced by the paralyzed man and his friends in Mark 2:1-12.

Just take a few suggestions, rather than running through the whole story, eg: nervous, helpless, confused, amazed.

Afterwards, explain that in all those different feelings, Jesus was fully in control. It's the same for us – we don't need to be afraid or impatient, and we can trust even when we don't understand, because Jesus is with us and has power over everything.

2. Why do you think Jesus forgives the man first? (Have another look at Mark 2:17.)

We would expect Jesus to have healed the man first, but Jesus knows that the man has a bigger problem. His greatest need is for his sins to be forgiven, so Jesus deals with this first. That is the main reason Jesus came – to provide a way for us to be forgiven instead of being punished as we deserve.

The aim of this question is to help the children understand that sin is a problem for them personally, as well as for others, and that God should rightly judge it.

If you have time, you may want to let the children do the puzzles on page 13, with some informal chat. If this is part of a holiday club or vacation Bible school, then the puzzle time is also a good opportunity to practise the memory verse and to plug any upcoming events or regular clubs.

Give out invitations to your family event.

3. Have a go at writing your own definition of the word "sin". Sin is...

Help the children see that sin isn't just about the wrong things we say and do, but it's also about our attitude towards God – the way we ignore him and disobey him, the way we don't treat him as we ought. If it has been used in the talk, you may want to refer back to the acrostic for sin:

Shove off God,
I'm in charge
Not you!

Sin is our biggest problem because it cuts us off from God.

4. Do you think that sin is a problem?

☐ **Sin isn't a problem.**

☐ **God should let us off every time we do something wrong.**

☐ **Sin spoils our world and should be punished.**

☐ **Something else...**

After they have ticked a box, ask the children to think about the problems they have with their friends, or about bigger problems such as war etc. We hurt people by our selfish behaviour. This is sin in action.

5. Can you think of ways you mess up or put yourself first? For example: cheat, lose your temper, etc? How would you feel if everyone could see all your wrong thoughts, words and actions?

Conclusion

Finish by encouraging your group members to come back next time. Tell them: "We've seen what sin is and why it is such a problem, but we've also discovered that Jesus came to deal with our problem. Next time we'll look at how he does that, so make sure you come back to explore the good news!"

Evaluate

- Is there anything you could add to your prayer cards? Was there anyone from the previous session missing today? You may be able to contact them and encourage them to come next time. If not, pray that they will return even without being contacted.

- Do you need to think about how to respond to any particular questions? Make sure you find time to plan your answer.

- Pray that the children will be convicted of their sin and their need of a Saviour.

(A downloadable version of these leader's notes for discussion groups is available from www.ceministries.org/epic.)

MYSTERIOUS MOUNTAINS
Jesus died in our place

Bible passage

Mark 15

Main aims

■ Children will know that Jesus' death was planned. He took the punishment we deserve for our sin.

■ Children will understand that through Jesus' death, there's now a way for us to be forgiven friends with God.

Session options

The following pages include a wide variety of activities. See pages 14-19 for suggestions of which activities to choose for different contexts or length of time.

Notes for leaders

📖 *Read Mark 15*

We pick up the crucifixion narrative at the point when Jesus has been taken by the Jewish leaders to be judged before Pilate, the Roman governor (verse 1). Just as with the high priest (Mark 14:61), Jesus remains silent (verses 4-5) and in doing so fulfils Isaiah 53:7. The only time Jesus does answer is to confirm his identity, his kingship (verse 2).

The answer Jesus gives rattles the religious leaders and there's a flurry of accusations. While Pilate knows that Jesus is innocent (verses 10, 14), he still opts to take the coward's way out and presents the crowd with the choice between a murderer (verse 7) or the King of the Jews. Who should be crucified? Who should be freed?

The scheming and manoeuvring of the religious leaders means the crowd yell for Barabbas to be released and Jesus to be condemned (verses 11-14). Motivated by the fear of a riot, Pilate sentences Jesus to flogging and death (verse 15). And so we see Mark 10:45 powerfully illustrated as the innocent one dies in the place of the guilty, and the guilty one goes free. What unfolds next is just as Jesus himself had foretold in 8:31, 9:31 and 10:33-34, and was prophesied in Psalm 22:1, 7, 18.

The identity of Jesus is ridiculed, as soldiers beat (Mark 15:19) and mock him: dressing him with a fake crown and robe (verse 17), paying him false homage (verses 18-19) and hanging a sarcastic sign above his head (verse 26). They are not alone in their scorn – passers-by (verse 29), the chief

Leader's checklist
Have you…

☐ Invited the children, and made clear the time and place where you will meet?

☐ Collected parental consent forms for any new children?

☐ Assigned leaders to the various activities and discussion groups?

☐ Prepared the talk, including any visual aids?

☐ Collected any items needed for the activities?

☐ *Epic Scratch Pads* (4-7s) and/or *Epic Logbooks* (8-11s) and a pencil for each child?

☐ Prepared the activities and questions for the discussion groups?

☐ Enough Bibles or Mark's Gospels for everyone, if you are using them?

☐ (Optional) Rehearsed the drama and collected props?

☐ Prayed for each group member and yourself as the leader?

priests (verse 31) and even the criminal on the cross next door (verse 32) deride his apparent inability to save himself. And yet the irony of their scoffing is that Jesus does indeed save others – but by *not* saving himself. He has to give himself as a ransom if he is to save others (Mark 10:45).

We see how it is that the cross saves others in verses 33-38. The darkness in the middle of the day is an indication of God's anger, since throughout the Old Testament darkness was a sign of God's judgment (eg: Exodus 10:21, Amos 8:9). On the cross, Jesus takes on our sin, and experiences the weight of God's wrath and judgment. He suffers the ultimate rejection as he is separated from his Father (verse 34) and then, after the price has been paid, he gives up his life voluntarily (verse 37).

The tearing of the temple curtain in two (verse 38) is a brilliant sign that Jesus' death means our sin has been dealt with – that we can now know forgiveness and reconciliation. Previously the temple curtain was like a big "no entry" sign, keeping worshippers in the temple out of the Most Holy Place and the presence of God. It was a sign that it is impossible for sinful people to approach a perfect God. The fact that God tore the curtain shows us that the way to God is now open, through Jesus. And to drive that point home, Mark quotes a Gentile centurion, charged with killing Jesus, who sees the evidence and believes that Jesus is God (verse 39, Mark 1:1).

Joseph of Arimathea, a secret disciple up to this point, boldly turns his back on the powerful Jewish council and approaches Pilate (verse 43). Pilate checked that Jesus was really dead (verses 44-45) and that security measures were put in place as he released the body (verse 46).

As Joseph buried Jesus, he must have wondered how the kingdom of God was going to come now. It must have seemed hopeless – and yet Jesus' work was complete. The price had been paid in full – so we do not need to do anything to earn our salvation. "Amazing love, how can it be, that you, my King, would die for me?"

Leader's prayer: Spend some time thanking God that Jesus did *not* save himself so that we could be saved; that he took God's wrath and died in our place. Praise God that we can know forgiveness and reconciliation through him.

MYSTERIOUS MOUNTAINS: TALK IDEA 1

Suitable for a holiday club or vacation Bible school, ages 4-11 or 8-11

You will need:
- A Roman soldier's costume to wear
- Sword
- Rope
- Chair, centre stage
- The Island map visual
- The "Breathtaking Bay" coloured visual
- The "Discovery Dens" coloured visual
- The "Mysterious Mountains" coloured visual*

* If you are combining sessions 3 and 4, you will also need the "Crown Cave" coloured visual.

This talk outline can also be downloaded from www.ceministries.org/epic

March on, centre stage.

I'm a solider, in charge of nearly 100 men, I'll have you know! And boy, I've seen a lot. The toughest place Caesar sent me was Jerusalem – not an easy job, believe me!

I mean, there was this one week which started off on a real high – tons of people turned out on the streets to…

Wave the rope in the air, like a sports supporters scarf.

… cheer on a guy called Jesus. He had been travelling round for a few years showing incredible power…

Stick up "Breathtaking Bay" visual.

… forgiving people…

Stick up "Discovery Dens" visual.

... and teaching about God. It seemed everyone loved him and yet, before the week was up, we were putting him to death on the Friday. Crazy!!!

We were brought in after the Jewish leaders had arrested Jesus during the night.

> Wrap rope round your wrists, and sit on the chair.

They didn't like the things Jesus was saying and doing, or the fact that he was so powerful and popular – and so they captured him and tried to find something they could punish him for. But do you know what? They couldn't – because he'd never done anything wrong!

However, when Jesus said he was God's chosen King and Son...

> Stand up, leaving the rope on the chair, and tap the crown on the "Breathtaking Bay" visual with the sword.

... the Jewish leaders decided he was lying, and could be punished for that. And so they started to beat him and laugh at him – and then they dragged him to see Governor Pilate.

> Move to the left side of the stage.

> Stand upright, with sword in front of chest and one hand cupped around your ear.

As I stood guard, I listened to Pilate questioning Jesus. But Jesus just remained quiet. Then he and another prisoner, called Barabbas, were taken onto the balcony.

> Step forward, to the very front of the stage.

By this time, there was quite a crowd gathered.

> Wave arm in front of you.

They were all keen to see...

> Stand on tiptoe, shielding eyes.

... what would happen to Jesus. Pilate silenced them.

> Finger on lips.

Then he gave them a choice – they had to choose who they wanted let go...

> Hold out right hand to your side.

... and who should be killed.

> Hold out left hand to your side.

In my mind it was a stupid thing to ask. Why on earth would they want Jesus killed? He hadn't done anything wrong. Why should he die in place of Barabbas, who was a thief and murderer?

But the crowd began to shout.

> Punch the air with your fist when talking about the crowd.

"Free Barabbas, kill Jesus! Free Barabbas, kill Jesus!" They got angrier and angrier. And Jesus...

> Stand with hands by your side.

... he just stood there, saying nothing. It was as if he knew what was going to happen.

My boss, Pilate, ordered that Jesus be killed, and so we led him away...

> Move back to centre stage.

... and gave him a beating.

> Pick up the rope and begin to whip.

When we were tired of whipping Jesus and mocking him, we tied a wooden beam to him.

> Drape the rope over your shoulders.

Then we lead him to a hillside.

> Drag the chair with you to the right side of the stage.

There, we nailed Jesus to a wooden cross...

> Stand on the chair, with arms outstretched.

... between two criminals, and gambled for his clothes to see who could keep them.

Now, I've seen many a man die on a cross – but never as Jesus did. He didn't scream or swear.

> Shake head.

Instead he forgave those who were being cruel to him. It was incredible. From the things I had heard, Jesus must have had the power to stop it all, to save himself, but he didn't. He stayed put.

He didn't deserve to die, but what could I do? It was my job to follow orders and so...

Climb off the chair and stand upright in front of it, tapping sword on your hand.

... I stood guard and I waited. I waited for him to die.

Pause.

Stopping tapping sword and slowing down speech for the next phrase:

And then the weirdest thing happened...

It was daytime, but all of a sudden it went pitch black. Total darkness in the middle of the day. For three hours!

Clutch sword in front of you, looking nervous.

None of it made sense, until Jesus cried out in a loud voice: "My God! Why have you turned away from me?"

God had turned away from his Son. Jesus took our punishment for the wrong we have done, and in doing so he was separated from his Father.

It should be us who are cut off from God, because we don't treat him the way we should. But Jesus died in our place. He died so that we can be forgiven friends with God for ever.

Stick "Mysterious Mountains" coloured visual on the map.

As Jesus took one last deep breath, he said: "It is finished" and died. The ground shook and a big, thick curtain in the temple tore in half. It was then I knew for certain that Jesus really was the Son of God.

Note: If you are combining sessions 3 and 4, use the alternative ending at the * below.

Move back to centre stage.

I wonder – who do you think Jesus is? Do you believe he's God's Son? Do you understand why he had to die?

– – – – – – – – – – –

* Alternative ending if you are combining sessions 3 and 4.

Pilate checked with us that Jesus was definitely dead. Then we gave his body to his friends, who wrapped him up and buried him in a tomb – a cave cut out of solid rock. A huge stone was pushed in front.

Mime pushing a stone.

Some of us soldiers were sent to guard the tomb.

Stand to attention.

There was no way anyone could get in or out.

And yet, Jesus did.

You see, a couple of days after he had died, Jesus came to life. Came as a bit of a shock to us all, I can tell you!

Sit on chair, looking surprised.

Jesus had promised it would happen, but no one really understood what he meant. Early on the Sunday morning, some women who were friends of Jesus discovered that the stone had been rolled away and his body had gone. An angel told them that Jesus had risen!

Stick up "Crown Cave" coloured visual.

He had done the impossible. He had died so we could be forgiven, and he had beaten death, showing us we can have life for ever with him. Jesus really is the Son of God.

Move back to centre stage.

I wonder – who do *you* think Jesus is? Do you believe he's God's Son? Do you understand why he had to die and then come to life?

MYSTERIOUS MOUNTAINS: TALK IDEA 2

Suitable for a mid-week club or children's Christianity Explored course, ages 8-11

You will need:

- Three story-picture cards (available to download from www.ceministries.org/epic):
  - 1: Jesus hanging on the cross
  - 2: the temple curtain ripping
  - 3: the Roman centurion
- A picture of a large calendar, with circled dates, to which you will add the 3 talk titles (download as above)
- A mobile/cell phone, with a "No Entry" sign on the back of it
- Items for your chosen method for telling the story (see below)
- "Sin" visuals from session 2 (see page 74), already displayed as a reminder of what we learned last time
- The Explorer Notebook (see page 156)

This talk outline can also be downloaded from www.ceministries.org/epic

Choose one of these three story options:

- *Either* show the Australian Bible Society videos on Mark 15 (there are two). Go to http://wild.biblesociety.org.au. Click on "Wild Teacher Resources" and then "Video Library". Watch both videos together, one after the other.

- *Or* have leaders perform an animated reading of Mark 15:22-39 with different leaders reading the parts of the various characters. Use whichever Bible version you are using with the group.

- *Or* summarize the verses and tell the story with some Bible pictures (download as above), eg:

1. Jesus was led up the hill dragging a cross, like a criminal, even though he had never done anything wrong. They nailed him to the cross, between two criminals, and gambled to win his clothes.

2. Then some of the people watching began to mock Jesus saying: "Ha, he said he was going to rescue others, but he can't even rescue himself" and: "Why don't you climb down and prove you're the Son of God?" Even those hanging on the crosses on either side joined in the insults.

3. In the middle of the day, when the sun should have been shining, the sky went dark and stayed dark for three hours. Jesus yelled out in an anguished voice: "My God, my God, why have you turned away from me?"

4. As Jesus breathed his last breath, the temple curtain ripped into two. The Roman centurion thought about all he had seen and heard, and he said: "Surely this man was the Son of God".

– – – – – – – – – – –

Hold up mobile/cell phone.

Imagine this phone has all the bad things I've ever done recorded on it. Or all the bad things you have ever done.

All the times you've lied and been rude to your parents. All the times you've picked on people, had a selfish thought and not treated God as you should. All your sin recorded. Imagine if I now uploaded it to *YouTube*! The embarrassment it would cause; the friendships it would spoil.

We heard last time that sin spoils our relationship with God (point to "It spoils") **and it separates us from God** (point to "It separates"). **I'm going to show you why.**

Imagine this hand is me – and the ceiling is where God is.

Put the phone on one hand.

This phone, which shows all my sin, is getting in the way between me and God. Our sin separates us from being God's friends and there's nothing we can do about it (point to "We're stuck").

Last time, we thought about the man who was lowered down through the roof, and we saw that Jesus forgave the man's sin. Jesus can do this because he is God's Son. But how can Jesus rescue us and forgive our sins? Well, it's all to do with the very special day when Jesus died.

1. A planned day

Stick up by the first circled date: "A planned day".

The day Jesus died was planned by God. There are lots of Bible verses that show us, but we'll stick with Mark. In Mark 8:31 it says: *"He then began to teach them that the Son of Man must suffer many things and be rejected by the elders, the chief priests and the teachers of the law, and that he must be killed and after three days rise again."*

Jesus knew that he was going to die. It wasn't an accident. He wasn't surprised when the religious leaders arrested him. He wasn't surprised when they handed him over to the Romans to be killed. He knew when and why he was going to die. He knew that it was part of God's rescue plan to save us from being stuck with the punishment we deserve.

Let's watch the videos/read the story before we think about why Jesus' death was the only way to save us.

Tell the story using one of the three story options on page 89.

2. A sad day

Stick up by the next circled date a label saying: "A sad day".

Hold up story picture 1.

What a shocking sight.

- The one who had taught about God with authority...
- The one who had healed so many...
- The one who had forgiven the paralyzed man...
- The one who had done nothing wrong – EVER...

... was being killed alongside two criminals.

Jesus didn't deserve to be punished but he chose to die in our place. He chose not to rescue himself, so we can be rescued.

Remember this phone with all my sin on, and how it separates me from God?

Hold up the phone and lay it flat on the same hand as before.

Now imagine this other hand is Jesus.

Hold up your other hand.

He never did anything wrong so there's nothing separating Jesus and his Father, God. But when Jesus died, he took all my sin...

Transfer phone from one hand to the other.

... and all of God's anger at sin was poured on his own Son, instead of on me.

That's why Jesus cried out: "God, why have you turned away from me?" God turned away from his Son for the only time ever as Jesus paid for our sin. It was the only way our sin problem could be fixed.

Now, look at my other hand. There's no barrier now – I'm no longer separated – because Jesus has taken my sin. That is how Jesus rescues us.

3. A happy day

Stick up by the last circled date: "A happy day".

The day Jesus died was a sad day because Jesus died a horrific death, but we call it *"Good* Friday" because it was also a happy day. It's happy because, through his death, Jesus did something amazing and wonderful.

Hold up story picture 2.

When Jesus died, the huge curtain in the temple ripped in two. God was using it as a big signpost to show us that now our sin has been dealt with, we can be God's forgiven friends. You see, in the past that big curtain had been like a giant "No Entry" sign into a place where people could meet God.

Show phone again, pointing to the "No Entry" sign on the back of it.

But when Jesus died, God tore the curtain to show that he had accepted Jesus' payment for our sin. Now, instead of being punished, we can be forgiven. Instead of death, we can know life. Instead of being stuck as God's enemies, we can be God's friends. All because of what Jesus has done.

Hold up story picture 3.

Some people in the crowd thought Jesus' death was a mistake. The religious leaders thought it was unnecessary. But the Roman soldier who was watching said that Jesus must be God's Son. I wonder what you think of Jesus' death?

The day that Jesus died was *a sad day* because Jesus, God's perfect Son, took our punishment. It was *a happy day* because Jesus died so that all who believe in him can be his forgiven friends. And it was *a planned day* – planned by God, as he'd always known it was the only way to rescue us.

Show page 3 of the Explorer Notebook: "and died in our place..."

Note: *If you are combining sessions 3 and 4, use the alternative ending at the* ***** *below.*

And another planned day was going to follow on the Sunday, because Jesus had promised he would come back to life on the third day. We'll think about that planned day next time.

– – – – – – – – – – –

* Alternative ending if you are combining sessions 3 and 4.

Another planned day was soon to follow on the Sunday, as Jesus had promised he would come back to life on the third day – and he did!

After Governor Pilate checked that Jesus was definitely dead, some good friends took Jesus' body away. They wrapped him in cloth and laid him in a tomb, which was blocked by a large stone and guarded by Roman soldiers.

Early on the Sunday morning, which was the third day, some of his friends returned to the tomb to put spices and perfume on Jesus' body. They would have felt as if it was another sad day...

Point to the visual of "a sad day".

... as they trudged towards the tomb, wondering how they could move the stone. But they didn't need to worry. It had already been moved! And it wasn't a sad day – it was a gloriously happy day...

Point to the visual of "a happy day".

... as they soon learned from an angel that Jesus had come back to life, just as he promised.

Point to the visual of "a planned day".

When Jesus came back to life, it showed again that Jesus is God's King and Son. He has the power to do what none of us can do. He can do the impossible, because nothing is impossible for God.

Jesus died and came alive, showing us that he is God's rescuing King, and showing us that one day he will return as God's judging King. He rules over everyone and he rules over everything, including death. Because Jesus beat death, we can beat death and live for ever.

This happy, planned day reminds us that his payment for our sin has been accepted, and now we can be God's forgiven friends. We'll find out how next time.

Ideas menu

INTRODUCTORY ACTIVITIES

Choose at least one of the following activities, to suit your group, your context and the time you have available. Most of the games can be adapted to work from the front or in a small-group setting.

Bridge the gap

Aim: To understand that sin separates us from God.

You will need two ropes, set out in two parallel lines with a gap between them.

1. Line the children up along the rope.

2. Explain that, when you give the signal, they must cross the gap, without stepping in-between the ropes.

3. After each crossing, separate the ropes further apart.

4. If the children step in the gap, they are out.

5. Keep playing until everyone is out.

Afterwards, explain that all of us say, think and do things that are wrong. All of us disobey God and don't treat him as we should. This separates us from God – it causes a big gap. But today we'll see how Jesus came to do something about the gap. He came to forgive us.

Swap, no swap

Aim: To see that when Jesus died, he made a great swap for us – he took our punishment and offers us his perfection.

You will need the "swap, no swap" PowerPoint slides (download from www.ceministries.org/epic).

1. Show the children a picture. They have to decide if they want to swap it for something else.

2. Some of the swaps will be better items, eg: swap sprouts for sweets; others will be worse eg: swap a palace for the slums.

At the end, explain that today we're going to hear about the greatest swap ever. We're going to hear how Jesus swapped all our badness for all his goodness. He took our punishment so we don't have to.

Hat quiz

Aim: To know that symbols may be linked to certain people.

You will need the hat quiz on page 16 of the *Epic Scratch Pad* (4-7s) or *Logbook* (8-11s).

1. Put children in small groups and have them turn to page 16 of their booklets.

2. Older children have to try to work out who wears each hat; whereas younger children can colour in two hats.

In the quiz, you can tell who someone is by the hat they wear. But Jesus was different. He came to rescue people, but didn't wear a fireman's helmet (4-7s). He was the King, but didn't wear a jewelled crown (8-11s).

Instead, there is something else – a symbol – that is often linked to Jesus. It shows us who he is and why he came. We're going to look at the cross and see what actually happened there.

Escape ball

Aim: To understand what a substitute is.

You will need at least one ball.

1. Children to stand in a circle – with legs apart and feet touching those on either side of them.

2. They are to try and stop the ball going through their legs, with one hand (the other hand needs to be behind their back).

3. If the ball goes through their legs, then they have to do a forfeit, eg: ten push ups, star jumps, squats, etc. But they can choose a leader to take the punishment for them. Once the forfeit has been taken, that child can re-join the game.

Explain that today we are going to see how Jesus died in our place and took our punishment.

MEMORY VERSE

Use it or lose it

The memory verse for the week is Mark 10:45.

"For even the Son of Man did not come to be served, but to serve, and to give his life as a ransom for many."

It's important that the verse is explained clearly and concisely, whether you teach a different section each day or teach the whole verse immediately (see page 62).

You will need:
- Words on PowerPoint or OHT so that you can display the verse via PowerPoint or overhead projector six or seven times, but with the font getting smaller and smaller each time. The words on the last slide should be almost unreadable.

1. Show the first slide and remind the children what the memory verse means; then teach actions for the different phrases:

    "For even" (hold up four fingers)

    "The Son of Man" (crown shape on top of head)

"Did not come" (wave arms so they criss-cross)

"To be served" (tapping own shoulders and looking smug)

"But to serve" (hold out arms in front, palms facing upwards)

"And to give his life" (arms out to the side, like on a cross)

"As a ransom for many" (act out counting money in one hand)

"Mark 10 verse 45" (hands cupped, in a book shape)

2. Ask the children to say the verse, with the actions. Then work through the slides with the children repeating the words each time. As the words get smaller, start to compliment the children on their eyesight and, after the final slide, challenge them to say it without any words whatsoever.

THEMED SNACK

Sad and smiley faces

You will need:
- Plain biscuits/cookies (eg: Rich Tea)
- Icing
- Sweets/lollies and other decorations

1. Give each child two biscuits/cookies.

2. They are to decorate one as a sad face and one as a smiley face.

3. As they decorate, remind the children that when Jesus died it *seemed* sad, but actually it was a happy day because he died to take our punishment so we can be God's friends.

PRAYER SUGGESTION

💬 *When you pray with the children, it is good to explain that "amen" means "I agree", and that it gives them the option of joining in.*

You will need:
- A sheet of paper for each child

1. Give each child a sheet of paper.

2. Ask them to think of something they want to say sorry to God for.

3. Ask them to imagine there's a picture of what they've done on their paper.

4. Then ask them to rip their paper in half*****.

5. Pray, thanking God for providing a way for us to be forgiven – that because of Jesus' death, we no longer have to be cut off from him.

6. Collect the paper and put it in the bin.

* Tearing the paper up is a picture of being forgiven if we trust in Jesus. But be careful the children don't think that ripping some paper in half means they are Christians!

CRAFT IDEAS

4-7s: Cross mosaics

You will need:
- Torn up bits of paper (about 1cm/½ inch square). Have a different container per colour, although it is good to have a mix of shades and patterns within each container.
- A4/US letter size paper
- PVA (white) glue and spreaders
- Cross template (download from www.ceministries.org/epic)

1. Ask the children to draw round the cross template onto a sheet of paper.

2. They then decide what colour they want to make their cross.

3. They spread glue on the cross and add on squares of paper in a mosaic fashion.

4. Keep going until the cross is complete.

5. Choose a contrasting colour to fill the outside of the paper.

6. You may want to write something on the paper at the end, eg: "It is finished".

4-11s: Cross photo clip stand

You will need:
- Lolly/popsicle sticks
- PVA (white) glue and spreaders
- Thin slips of white paper, like a banner
- Air-hardening clay (green if possible)
- Brown felt-tip pens
- DIY photo clip holders (available from online craft stores)

1. Give each child a lump of clay to mould into a mound.

2. Colour the two lolly/popsicle sticks brown.

3. Glue the sticks together into a cross shape.

4. Have the children write on the banner: "Jesus died to save me".

5. Stick the banner to the horizontal bar of the cross.

6. Wedge the cross into the mound.

7. Stick the photo clip holder into the mound, behind the cross.

8. Encourage the children to put a photo of themselves in the clip, to remind them that Jesus died for them.

4-11s: Suncatcher cross

You will need:
- Photocopies of a cross outline on clear acetate sheets
- Squares of tissue paper
- PVA (white) glue and spreaders
- Scissors
- Black permanent marker pens

1. Glue pieces of tissue paper onto the acetate within the cross outline.

2. Go round the outline with a permanent marker.

3. Cut out the cross shape, and explain to the children that they can stick it to their window.

8-11s: Paid in full

You will need:
- Paper plates
- Red, orange, yellow and purple paint
- Sticky glue dots
- Fake coins or plenty of pennies
- Black paper
- Chalk
- Scissors
- Paint brushes
- Water pots
- Stapler

1. Ask the children to paint the paper plate as if it was a sunset sky.

2. While the plate is drying, give them a sheet of black paper and ask them to cut out a silhouette of a hillside with three crosses on it.

3. On the middle cross, glue some coins.

4. Beneath the cross, on the hillside, write in chalk: "Paid in full".

5. Staple the black paper to the paper plate to complete the sunset scene.

TEAM CHALLENGE

Cream mountain

You will need:
- Cans of squirty cream
- Grapes
- Paper plates
- Paper towels

1. Ask for a volunteer from each team.

2. Give them each a paper plate; then place a grape on it.

3. Squirt cream over the grape into a mountain shape.

4. It is the first child to stick their head into cream and eat their grape that wins.

DRAMA

In today's drama, the three remaining Epic Explorers (Crop, Sonny and Berry) find a tree that's been split in half by lightning. They follow the path through the tree, Sonny finds the next clue, and they set off for Crown Cave. See page 148.

EPIC SCRATCH PAD
DISCUSSION GROUPS FOR 4-7s

Bible passage: Mark 15

Main aims

- Children will know that Jesus' death was planned. He took the punishment we deserve for our sin.
- Children will understand that through Jesus' death, there's now a way for us to be forgiven friends with God.

Introduction

- Welcome the children back.
- Learn the names of any new children.
- Remind them of your name.
- Recap on previous session, eg: "Last time, we saw that Jesus came to deal with our biggest problem, our problem of sin. We thought about the fact that *all* of us sin – all of us do things wrong, say things wrong and think things wrong. All of us disobey God, ignore him and don't treat him as we ought to. We also began to think about the fact that sin is such a serious problem because it separates us from God for ever. We deserve the punishment of hell, but Jesus came to rescue us from the punishment we deserve."
- "This time we're going to find out what happened when Jesus died and how he rescues us."

Booklet

If there's time and it's one of your chosen introductory activities, complete "Hat quiz" on page 16 of the *Scratch Pad*. (See page 92 of this Leader's Guide for how to run this activity.)

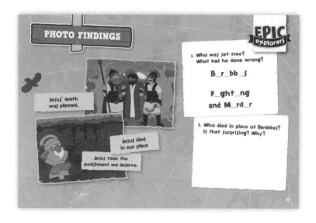

Photo findings

The recap below (called "Photo findings") appears on page 17 of the *Epic Scratch Pad*. It is a simple storyboard with the teaching summarized.

- Jesus' death was planned.
- Jesus died in our place.
- Jesus took the punishment we deserve.

As you look at the pictures, if you have time, you could ask the children to tell you if they remember what is happening.

Questions

Use the questions to encourage discussion.

1. Who was set free? What had he done wrong?

Ask the children if they can remember who the baddie in the story was, who was then set free. You may need to prompt them, eg: "sounds a bit like 'Barry'". After the children have filled in what Barabbas had done wrong, it would be good to point out that even though we may not be exactly the same, we do still do wrong things... AND think wrong things... AND say wrong things... AND disobey God... and so we deserve to be punished by God. Link to when we disobey our teachers or parents – they punish us because we deserve it.

2. Who died in place of Barabbas? Is that surprising? Why?

A nice, easy question that pretty much everyone should be able to answer... JESUS! Ask the children to think about why it is surprising. For the previous two sessions we've focussed on the fact Jesus is God's Son, the miracle worker, who cares for our needs and is hugely popular – and now he's been arrested and killed. Even though he has so much power, he didn't struggle or stop the arrest. Then explain it wasn't a surprise to Jesus – he actually knew about it all. It was planned to the tiniest detail since before time began!

3. Who did Jesus die for? Why?

Use this question to help children understand that we *all* deserve to be punished. No one is so "good" that they don't need forgiveness; and no one is so "bad" that they can't be forgiven. Jesus took God's punishment for everyone who trusts in him. He died in our place, so we can be forgiven and become his friend for ever.

A visual illustration will help the children understand why we need to be forgiven – see below or page 100. (If you used Talk Idea 2 (page 89), this will be a recap of the phone illustration.)

Show the group your right hand. Explain that your hand stands for you, and the ceiling stands for God. Show a book (not the Bible) and ask them to imagine it contains a record of your sin – every time you have said, thought or done things that are wrong. Put the book flat on your hand.

Ask: "What does the book do?" (It separates us from God and stops us knowing him as our friend.)

Now hold up your left hand – this stands for Jesus. Explain that Jesus lived a perfect life; he never sinned – so there was nothing separating him from God. Explain that, as Jesus died on the cross, the sin of the whole world was put onto him. Transfer the book from your right to your left hand to show this.

Ask: "What is there between Jesus and God?" (The book that lists all your sin.) This is why Jesus died – it was to take the punishment for all our sin. Then look at your right hand and ask: "What is there between me and God?" (Nothing!)

When Jesus died on the cross, he took the punishment for our sins so that we can be forgiven. This means that there is nothing to separate us from God anymore. This was God's rescue plan for us!

4. **Jesus died to take our punishment so that we can be forgiven. Draw what happened to the temple curtain, to show we now can be friends with God…**

After the children have drawn a rip in the temple curtain, discuss with them the fact that there is no longer a barrier between us and God (refer back to previous session). Hold a piece of paper in front of your face. Talk about how you are separated from the children. But then rip it in half. What is getting in the way now? Nothing! And as a result of Jesus paying the price for our sin, nothing need get in the way between us and God.

5. **Which group of people in the story are you most like? Do you think:**

   ☐ **Yes, Jesus is King. I want to follow him.**

   ☐ **Ha Ha! It's all rubbish!**

   ☐ **Ummm… I think I need to know more.**

After they have chosen their response, ask if any of the group want to share their answer. Be prepared to open up the discussion or revisit it tomorrow. Again, this question gives you the opportunity not only to see where the children are at, but also to share something of your own testimony.

If you have time, you may want to let the children do the puzzles on page 19, with some informal chat. If this is part of a holiday club or vacation Bible school, then the puzzle time is also a good opportunity to practise the memory verse and to plug any upcoming events or regular clubs.

Give out invitations to your family event.

Conclusion
Finish by encouraging your group members to come back next time. Tell them: "We've seen why Jesus' death is so important to Christians. But what happened next? Well, the Bible tells us that Jesus came back to life. Next time we're going to think a little more about that and why it matters."

Evaluate
- Is there anything you could add to your prayer cards? Was there anyone from the previous session missing today? You may be able to contact them and encourage them to come next time. If not, pray that they will return even without being contacted.

- Do you need to think about how to respond to any particular questions? Make sure you find time to plan your answer.

- Pray that the children will understand why Jesus had to die and what this amazing rescue plan means for them.

(A downloadable version of these leader's notes for discussion groups is available from www.ceministries.org/epic.)

EPIC LOGBOOK
DISCUSSION GROUPS FOR 8-11s

Bible passage: Mark 15

Main aims

- Children will know that Jesus' death was planned. He took the punishment we deserve for our sin.
- Children will understand that through Jesus' death, there's now a way for us to be forgiven friends with God.

Introduction

- Welcome the children back.

- Learn the names of any new children.

- Remind them of your name.

- Recap on previous session, eg: "Last time, we saw that Jesus came to deal with our biggest problem, our problem of sin. We thought about the fact that *all* of us sin – all of us do things wrong, say things wrong and think things wrong. All of us disobey God, ignore him and don't treat him as we ought to. We also began to think about the fact that sin is such a serious problem because it separates us from God for ever. We deserve the punishment of hell, but Jesus came to rescue us from the punishment we deserve."

- "This time we're going to find out what happened when Jesus died and how he rescues us."

Booklet

If there's time and it's one of your chosen introductory activities, complete "Hat quiz" on page 16 of the *Logbook*. (See page 92 of this Leader's Guide for how to run this activity.)

Explorer's entries

The recap below (called "Explorer's entries") appears on page 17 of the *Epic Logbook*. If you have time, you may want to read through and summarize.

- Mark 8:31 – Jesus' death was planned.

- Mark 15:22-39 - Jesus died to take the punishment we deserve. He died in our place.

- Mark 15:22-39 – Jesus died so that we can be God's forgiven friends.

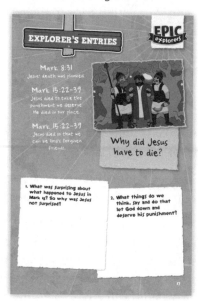

Questions

Use the questions to encourage discussion.

1. What was surprising about what happened to Jesus in Mark 15? So why was Jesus not surprised?

Jesus – the perfect one, God's Son, the miracle worker followed by crowds – was arrested and killed. This surprise should contrast sharply with the fact that Jesus didn't struggle, and actually knew about it all in advance. It was planned to the tiniest detail since before time began!

2. What things do we think, say and do that deserve God's punishment?

The children may write a few things or lots. Either way, it's good to point out that we all still do wrong things... AND think wrong things... AND say wrong things... AND disobey God... and so we deserve to be punished by God – leaders as well as children. Link to when they disobey their teachers or parents, or when we get caught speeding by a policeman. They punish us because we deserve it (an opportunity to recap on yesterday).

3. How would you feel if someone else deliberately took the punishment for something you had done?

☐ **Smug – they're a fool for taking the blame.**

☐ **Guilty – I should have been punished instead.**

☐ **Bad – for the person who suffered.**

☐ **Grateful – thankful for the person who took my punishment.**

☐ **Or a mix of these?**

Afterwards, you may want to discuss with the children how they would feel if it was a really serious punishment, eg: going to prison. This should help them begin to think about guilt, fairness, responsibility, etc. There is therefore no need to comment on their replies.

4. **What brilliant things will happen when Jesus takes the punishment for someone's sins?**

Answers may include:

- They will see God's love and power at work.
- They will be forgiven .
- They will become God's friends.
- They will look forward to living with God in heaven for ever.

If you have done the talk with the phone illustration and the "no entry" sign (page 89), you could recap on that now.

If you have had the soldier's monologue (page 86), then a visual illustration here would be helpful to make sure the children understand why we need to be forgiven – see below or page 100.

Show the group your right hand. Explain that your hand stands for you, and the ceiling stands for God. Show a book (not the Bible) and ask them to imagine it contains a record of your sin – every time you have said, thought or done things that are wrong. Put the book flat on your hand.

Ask: "What does the book do?" (It separates us from God and stops us knowing him as our friend.)

Now hold up your left hand – this stands for Jesus. Explain that Jesus lived a perfect life; he never sinned – so there was nothing separating him from God. Explain that, as Jesus died on the cross, the sin of the whole world was put onto him. Transfer the book from your right to your left hand to show this.

Ask: "What is there between Jesus and God?" (The book that lists all your sin.) This is why Jesus died – it was to take the punishment for all our sin. Then look at your right hand and ask: "What is there between me and God?" (Nothing!)

(A downloadable version of these leader's notes for discussion groups is available from www.ceministries.org/epic.)

When Jesus died on the cross, he took the punishment for our sins so that we can be forgiven. This means that there is nothing to separate us from God anymore. This was God's rescue plan for us!

5. **Which of the reactions to Jesus' death is most like your own? Why?**

☐ **The confused crowd – you don't understand.**

☐ **The religious leaders – you don't need Jesus' help .**

☐ **The Roman Soldier – wow! Jesus must be God!**

After the children have chosen their responses, ask if any of them want to share their answer. Be prepared to open up the discussion or revisit it tomorrow. This question gives you the opportunity not only to see where the children are at in their understanding and response, but also to share something of your own testimony.

If you have time, you may want to let the children do the crossword on page 19, with some informal chat. If this is part of a holiday club or vacation Bible school, then the puzzle time is also a good opportunity to practise the memory verse and to plug any upcoming events or regular clubs.

Give out invitations to your family event.

Conclusion

Finish by encouraging your group members to come back next time. Tell them: "We've seen why Jesus' death is so important to Christians. But what happened next? Well, the Bible tells us that Jesus came back to life. Next time we're going to think a little more about that and why it matters."

Evaluate

- Is there anything you could add to your prayer cards? Was there anyone from the previous session missing today? You may be able to contact them and encourage them to come next time. If not, pray that they will return even without being contacted.

- Do you need to think about how to respond to any particular questions? Make sure you find time to plan your answer.

- Pray that the children will understand why Jesus had to die and what this amazing rescue plan means for them.

The book/phone illustration

This illustration can be helpful when explaining what happened when Jesus was dying on the cross.

What to do	**What to say**

What to do

What to say

Hold up a book (not the Bible) or a mobile/cell phone in your right hand.

Imagine that someone has written about your life in this book (or filmed your life on this mobile/cell phone) – but they've just chosen the bad stuff. Every time you've told a lie. Each time you let a friend down or were rude to your mum or dad. All the times you laughed at someone behind their back or took something that wasn't yours.

So this is a record of your sin – every time you have said, thought or done things that are wrong.

Hold your left hand out, with your palm facing the ceiling.

Imagine that this hand is me, and that the ceiling is where God is.

Take the book/phone and put it flat on your hand.

This book/phone shows all the wrong stuff I've ever done – it shows my sin.

Ask: "But when I put it here *(on your hand),* what does it do?" (It gets in the way between me and God.)

It stops me from knowing God and living as his friend. That's why sin is such a problem – it separates us from God.

Hold out your right hand, facing up. Your left hand should still have the book/phone.

Imagine that this hand is Jesus. He was perfect. He never did anything wrong – he never sinned. That means that there was nothing at all between Jesus and his Father, God. They had a perfect, loving relationship.

But when Jesus was dying on the cross, this is what happened:

Now transfer the book/DVD from the left hand to the right hand.

Ask: "What is there between Jesus and God?" (The book/phone that lists all your sin.)

This is why Jesus died – it was to take the punishment for all our sin.

Refer to your left hand, now empty, still facing upwards.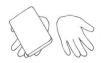

But look back at my other hand for a moment.

Ask: "What is there between me and God?" (Nothing!)

When Jesus died on the cross, he took the punishment for our sins so that we can be forgiven. This means that there is nothing to separate us from God anymore. This was God's rescue plan for us!

CROWN CAVE
Jesus is alive and offers new life

Bible passage
Mark 16:1-8

Main aims
- Children will know that Jesus really did die and rise again.
- Children will understand that, because Jesus has beaten death, we can know life in him.

Session options
The following pages include a wide variety of activities. See pages 14-19 for suggestions of which activities to choose for different contexts or length of time.

Notes for leaders
📖 *Read Mark 16:1-8*

Conspiracy theories are very popular, aren't they? And as people look to explain away why Jesus' tomb was empty that first Easter, a number of alternatives to him rising again have been cited over the years: maybe the body was stolen, or perhaps Jesus didn't really die. Mark, however, wants us to be in no doubt whatsoever that Jesus definitely was dead, and definitely rose from the dead – so Mark gives us a number of eye-witness accounts.

Eyewitness evidence 1:
We saw in the last session that Jesus was definitely dead (Mark 15:42-47). Pilate had checked with the centurion who saw Jesus die, and he confirmed it. As renowned executioners, the Romans did not make mistakes.

Eyewitness evidence 2:
The two women who saw where Jesus was buried (Mark 15:47) were also totally persuaded that he was dead. They would not have bothered buying expensive spices to anoint a corpse (Mark 16:1) if they had not been convinced Jesus was dead.

Eyewitness evidence 3:
When the three women got to the tomb, however, they saw that the stone had moved (verse 4); Jesus was not there (verse 6); and that there was an angel in the tomb (verse 5). Unsurprisingly, the women were filled with fear – but they didn't need to be. The angel had come to tell them the greatest news ever – Jesus had been crucified, but had

---

Leader's checklist
Have you...

- ☐ Invited the children, and made clear the time and place where you will meet?
- ☐ Collected parental consent forms for any new children?
- ☐ Assigned leaders to the various activities and discussion groups?
- ☐ Prepared the talk, including any visual aids?
- ☐ Collected any items needed for the activities?
- ☐ *Epic Scratch Pads* (4-7s) and/or *Epic Logbooks* (8-11s) and a pencil for each child?
- ☐ Prepared the activities and questions for the discussion groups?
- ☐ Enough Bibles or Mark's Gospels for everyone, if you are using them?
- ☐ (Optional) Rehearsed the drama and collected props?
- ☐ Prayed for each group member and yourself as the leader?

risen from the dead, and they would see him alive again. Not only that, but it had all happened "just as he told you" (Mark 8:31, 9:31, 10:33. Jesus has again proved he is God's only chosen King and Son (Mark 1:1).

This is news worth passing on, and that's exactly what the angel urges the women to do (verse 7), despite the disciples' earlier disbelief and failures. The special mention of Peter reminds us of the wonderful hope we have in the gospel. Peter, the one who had been full of pride and false promises, (14:31), and yet denied Jesus (14:66-72), could now be restored and forgiven. We too can repent and believe the good news (1:14-15), and know the sweetness of Jesus' forgiveness and the power of his transformation.

And so the challenge is: have the children responded to the risen Jesus? Have they sought new life in him? Do they think following him is worth it? And if so, will they go? Will they tell others? Or will they show fear rather than faith, as in verse 8?

Leader's prayer: Praise God that death is defeated and victory is won. Thank him for the hope we have in the gospel. Pray that he will help us unashamedly teach the gospel, and to please bring others into his kingdom.

CROWN CAVE: TALK IDEA 1

Suitable for a holiday club or vacation Bible school, ages 4-11 or 8-11

You will need:

- Two actors to play the Roman centurion and Mary Magdalene
- Detective's costume with magnifying glass
- Detective's notebook
- Large "stone" (large beach ball or something bigger if possible)
- Fold-up cardboard spear
- White cloth
- Perfume bottle
- Briefcase, which has all the clues in apart from the stone
- Soldier's costume
- Headscarf for Mary
- The Island map visual with the "Breathtaking Bay", "Discovery Dens" and "Mysterious Mountains" coloured visuals all stuck on
- The "Crown Cave" coloured visual.

This talk outline can also be downloaded from www.ceministries.org/epic

Detective tiptoes on wearing costume, carrying a briefcase and magnifying glass, peering around.

Detective: **A-ha, what do we have here? Children – and lots of them! Fantastic, you can help me solve the mystery of the missing body. Have you heard that Jesus has died?**

Point to the "Mysterious Mountains" section on the map.

Well, his body was buried in a stone tomb, a bit like a cave – but now it's been reported that Jesus' tomb is empty. But how's that possible? Has his body been stolen? Did he not really die? Or has he actually come to life?

I've been using my detective skills to collect clues from around the tomb.

Pop open the briefcase and start pulling the clues out.

So, we have here a spear, white rags, a perfume jar and a big rock (roll out from the set nearby). **But I must admit, I can't really make sense of the evidence. What I need is to interview some people who were actually there – some eye-witnesses.**

Enter Roman centurion, wearing the same costume as in talk 3, and marching.

Roman centurion: **Left, right, left, right, left, right.**

Stops and salutes the detective.

Detective: **Good day, sir. How very nice to meet you. I was wondering if you could help me? I'm trying to solve the mystery of Jesus' missing body. Can you tell me – did Jesus definitely die?**

Roman centurion: **Well of course he did, young man. No doubt about it. We Romans are excellent executioners, you know, and we weren't about to make a mistake this time. We double checked, by sticking a spear through his heart, before we sent word he was dead.**

Detective: **Ok, so Jesus definitely died – but what happened next? Was his body definitely put in the tomb?**

Roman Centurion: **Oh yes. After Governor Pilate spoke with me, Jesus' body was wrapped up and taken away by an important-looking fellow. Joseph was his name. He put the body in a brand-new tomb, which some of my men were sent to guard – making sure no one could get in.**

Detective: (musing) **Interesting… So that would explain why there is a spear there. But then what happened? Where's the body?**

Roman centurion: **I don't know – but one thing I do know is Jesus is the Son of God, so he had the power to do any-**

thing. Anyway, best be off – orders to give, places to march. Left, right, left, right, left, right.

Roman centurion departs, and Mary Magdalene runs on, looking excited and as if she's trying to find people.

Detective: Er, excuse me, madam. I wonder if you could help me? I'm trying to find out what has happened to Jesus' body. I have some clues here but I don't really know what they mean.

Mary Magdalene: (excitedly) **Jesus' body? I can tell you! I was there when Joseph wrapped him in cloth and buried him. See this stone** (point at it)? **The Romans rolled this into the entrance to make sure no one could get in.**

Detective: Really? You saw him dead and buried? You saw this rock in front of his tomb? What did you say your name is?

Mary Magdalene: **My name is Mary Magdalene, and oh yes, he was dead. That's why my friends and I collected together our money so we could go and buy some spices and perfume** (point to the bottle) **to put on the body.**

Detective: Thank you Mary. Let me just get this straight… you're telling me that Jesus' body was placed in the tomb, and as well as soldiers standing guard, this big stone was put in front? But this stone wasn't in front of the tomb when I found it.

Mary Magdalene: (in an excitable voice) **Well, of course it wasn't! When Mary, Salome and I went to the tomb very early on Sunday morning, we were worried about how we would move the heavy stone. But when we got there, it had already been rolled away.**

Detective: So what did you do?

Mary Magdalene: **We went in. Can you imagine our amazement when we discovered Jesus' body was no longer there? There were just these cloths he'd been wrapped in** (hold up the cloths)**. We**

were even more amazed when we saw a man in white sitting there. He was an angel, who…

Detective: Wait. Hold fire. You saw an angel? You all actually SAW an angel?!

Mary Magdalene: **Yes, and we spoke with him too. He knew we were looking for Jesus but he told us Jesus wasn't in the tomb as he had risen from the dead! And then the angel reminded us that Jesus had promised this would all happen.**

I didn't know what to make of it at first. In fact, I was so scared I ran away. But Jesus is alive! It's incredible; it's amazing; it's fantastic. I hope you don't mind, but I have to go. I need to tell the others, especially Peter – the angel asked me to pass on this great news.

Mary Magdalene dashes off.

Detective: **Wow! Astonishing. I now feel I have enough evidence to solve the mystery of the missing body. There's only one explanation – Jesus really has risen from the dead!**

Stick up the "Crown Cave" coloured visual.

And if Jesus has the power to do that – to beat death, to do the impossible – he really must be God's Son and the King of everything.

Look at notebook.

So let me get this right. On the Mysterious Mountains, we saw that Jesus died to take our punishment; and now at Crown Cave, God is showing he's accepted that rescue by giving Jesus new life. Woah, hang on! That means, if our punishment's been taken by Jesus, we can be forgiven and not separated from God, which means… we can have new life too; we can live for ever with God. Amazing! I've got to find out more right now…

Detective runs off.

CROWN CAVE:
TALK IDEA 2

Suitable for a mid-week club or children's Christianity Explored course, ages 8-11

You will need:

- 2 "crime scene" pictures – the illustrations for this talk are all available to download from www.ceministries.org/epic
- The Explorer Notebook (see page 156)
- A table
- 3 box files, each with one of these questions stuck onto it: "Was Jesus dead?", "Was Jesus alive?" and "Does it really matter?"
- Labels to stick onto the box files saying: "Definitely dead", "Definitely alive", and "Definitely matters"

- **In the "Was Jesus dead?" file:**
  - A helmet with a tag saying: "Brilliant executioner"
  - Some white strips of cloth, tied with a tag saying: "Tightly bound, and buried by friends"
  - A picture of some soldiers guarding the tomb, labelled: "The Romans made sure"

- **In the "Was Jesus alive?" file:**
  - A large stone with a tag saying: "The stone had been moved"
  - An angel Christmas decoration, with a tag saying: "The angel said so"
  - Lots of figure people (eg: Lego, Playmobil), with a sign to place by them saying: "People saw him and were prepared to die for him"

- **In the "Does it really matter?" file:**
  - A crown with a tag saying: "Jesus is God's Son. He is King of everything."
  - A victory poster with the label: "Jesus beat death"
  - A pocket mirror with a tag saying: "We can beat death"

This talk outline can also be downloaded from www.ceministries.org/epic

How good are you at solving mysteries? Look at the picture – can you work out what has happened?

Have on the screen a picture of a "crime scene", eg: a room turned upside down.

Take a few responses. Then ask:

What about this picture? Can anyone tell me one unusual thing?

Show a picture of the empty tomb, and take a couple of responses. If it appears a child wants to retell the whole account, then gently interrupt and thank them for their contribution.

A good detective needs to be someone who can carefully examine the scene, follow up what the eyewitnesses saw, and use clues to solve the mystery.

That's what we're going to do today. We're going to examine the scene of Jesus' tomb, discover what the eyewitnesses saw, and then use the clues to work out if Jesus came alive, and why it matters so much. But before we do, let's remind ourselves of our discoveries so far.

Hold up the Explorer Notebook and turn to the appropriate pages while you recap.

We have seen so far that Jesus is the Son of God, who is able to forgive sins and died in our place. And yet in the 2nd picture, the tomb was empty; there was no body there. So, was Jesus definitely dead when they put him inside?

Hold up box file 1 with the question "Was Jesus dead?" stuck on the outside.

1. Definitely dead
On the Friday night, after Jesus had died, an important man called Joseph of Arimathea went to see Governor Pilate and asked to bury Jesus' body.

- Read Mark 15:44-45

Who did Pilate check with to make absolutely certain that Jesus was dead? (Take responses.) That's right, he asked the Roman centurion, who had seen Jesus die with his very own eyes.

Pull out either a centurion's helmet or a picture of a centurion, with a tag saying: "Brilliant executioner" and hold it up.

Pilate believed the centurion, because he knew his soldiers were brilliant executioners (show tag) – they didn't make mistakes. So, Pilate agreed that Joseph could take the body.

But here's more evidence to help answer the question: Was Jesus dead?

Pull out strips of white cloth, with a tag saying: "Tightly bound, and buried by friends".

Joseph wrapped Jesus' body tightly in cloth, like an Egyptian mummy, and placed him in the stone tomb. To make sure no one could get in, Pilate had a huge stone pushed across the entrance. All of this was seen by Jesus' friends, the two Marys.

So was Jesus dead? Well, he had been killed by a brilliant executioner (hold up clue 1), he had been buried by good friends (hold up clue 2), and there's one more thing…

Take out the picture of Roman soldiers guarding the tomb.

Highly trained Roman soldiers were sent to seal the tomb and guard it with their lives. They were to make sure that no one went in or out of the tomb. So, was Jesus dead?

Hold up box file 1.

Yes! Definitely!

On top of the question: "Was Jesus dead?", stick the statement: "Definitely dead".

Now usually, this is where a book about someone's life would finish. The next words we'd expect to find would be: "The end". Except this is no ordinary story; this is no ordinary man. We've already seen this in the life Jesus led and in the death he died. And now, we're about to see it all over again as we start the final chapter of Mark and we try to answer our next question: Was Jesus alive?

Hold up second box file, showing the question: "Was Jesus alive?"

2. Definitely alive

It was dawn on the Sunday morning when three women crept to the tomb. That's the scene in our picture earlier. They wanted to put spices on Jesus' dead body to stop it smelling, even though they weren't sure how they could move the huge stone. But it turned out they didn't need to worry.

- Read Mark 16:4

As the women arrived, they saw that the stone had been rolled away.

Pull out a stone from the box file with a tag attached saying: "The stone had been moved". Have a volunteer read the tag.

Why is it incredible that the stone had been moved? (Take ideas, eg: it was so heavy, the Romans were guarding it, etc.)

But that wasn't the only thing the women saw, because now they could see into the tomb and there was a surprising sight. Listen to verse 5 and try to spot what that was.

- Read Mark 16:5

The women saw an angel – a messenger from God.

Pull out an angel Christmas decoration from the box with the tag: "The angel said so".

The angel told them (show tag) that Jesus had risen from the dead just as he had promised he would. He was alive and they would soon see him. In fact, we read in other eyewitness accounts that lots of people saw Jesus after he died and came to life.

Take out from the box lots of little people figures (eg: Playmobil) one after another.

Put a sign in front of the play figures saying: "People saw him and were prepared to die for him".

People talked and walked with Jesus, ate with him and hugged him. They were so certain that Jesus was alive that they told everyone – and many of them were even prepared to die for insisting he was alive. How amazing is that?

So was Jesus alive? Well, we know the stone was moved; an angel was in the tomb and said Jesus had risen just as he promised; and people saw Jesus and died for him. Was Jesus alive?

Yes! Definitely!

Stick the statement: "Definitely alive" over the question: "Was Jesus alive?"

Jesus definitely died and definitely is alive, but why does it matter?

Hold up third box file, showing the question: "Does it really matter?"

3. Definitely matters

Pull out a crown, with the tag saying: "Jesus is God Son. He is King of everything."

When Jesus rose from the dead, it showed again that he is God's Son and King of everything (show page 1 of the Explorer Notebook). **If he had stayed dead, his death would be like the normal death of any human. But in rising again, Jesus shows he is both fully man and the Son of God, with the power to rise from the dead. Nothing is impossible for Jesus, because he rules over all.**

Pull out a victory poster.

We thought last time about how Jesus took our punishment; how he paid the price for our sin by dying (show page 3 of the Explorer Notebook). **If Jesus had stayed dead, he would still be under the punishment for our sin, but**

in Mark 16, God shows he has accepted that payment by bringing Jesus to life (show page 4 of the Explorer Notebook). **Jesus had victory over sin and death!**

Pull out a pocket mirror, with the tag: "We can beat death". Hold it in front of a few children so they can see their reflection.

And that's not all. Just as God gave Jesus new life, he also promises new life to those who believe Jesus died for them and who live his way. Through Jesus, we can be forgiven and know God's power – the same power that raised Jesus – at work in us.

We deserve to be separated from God for ever, but Jesus rising again shows us that God will give us life after we die; life for ever with him. That's why the angel told the women to go and tell others.

So does it really matter that Jesus definitely died (tap first box file) **and is definitely alive** (tap second box file)**?**

Yes! Definitely!

Stick over the question on the third box file, the statement: "Definitely matters".

It absolutely matters because:

- **we see God's power**

- **we see that Jesus' payment for our sin has been accepted and he has victory over death**

- **and we see that through him, we can live with him for ever.**

Ideas menu

INTRODUCTORY ACTIVITIES

Choose at least one of the following activities, to suit your group, your context and the time you have available. Most of the games can be adapted to work from the front or in a small-group setting.

Just a minute

Aim: To begin to think about how we know something is true.

You will need a timer.

1. Choose a volunteer to come to the front. They have to speak for a minute without repetition or hesitation. Each topic begins with: "How would you prove that _____ is true?"

2. Have different topics, eg: How would you prove the world isn't flat?, How would you prove that chocolate tastes great?, How would you prove that red and yellow make orange?

At the end, say that today we're going to be thinking about a bigger question: "How can we prove that Jesus came back to life?" We will discover that there's lots of evidence.

Eyewitness

Aim: To introduce the idea of an eyewitness giving details about what they have seen.

You will need a tray with ten objects on it, eg: a ball, a fork, a pencil sharpener, etc., and something to cover the tray.

1. Ask the children to look at the items on the tray for a short period of time.

2. Cover up the tray and see what the children can remember.

Afterwards, explain that they looked carefully to take in the details; they were eyewitnesses of what was on the tray. And today we're going to meet some eyewitnesses of Jesus' grave; they, too, looked carefully at the details.

Spot the difference

Aim: To start to think about examining a scene and identifying clues.

You will need the *Epic Scratch Pads* and/or *Logbooks*.

1. There is a "spot the difference" puzzle on page 22 of the children's booklets. Ask the children to complete this on their own or in pairs.

2. Go through the answers.

Afterwards, congratulate them on looking so closely at the scene. Explain that today we're going to look closely at the scene of Jesus' grave – and it may look a little different to what they expect.

Opposites

Aim: To see that though Jesus died, he was alive – and what seemed like bad news is actually great news.

1. Have the children line up, side by side, at one end of the room and explain that you are going to play "opposites".

2. You say a word; and the first person to reply with the correct opposite takes a step forward.

3. The first person to reach you wins.

At the end, explain that we will see lots of opposites in today's true story. People will go from being sad to happy, as Jesus will go from being dead to being alive. Challenge them to see if they can spot any more opposites in the story.

List of opposites:
- Big – little
- Old – new
- Dark – light
- Before – after
- Sad – happy
- Empty – full
- Forget – remember
- Hard – easy
- Enemy – friend
- Dead - alive

MEMORY VERSE

Treasure map

You will need:

- A card island with the memory-verse words written clearly on it (see page 153). Cut the island into jigsaw pieces.
- Blu-tack reuseable adhesive
- A pirate hat and patch

1. Have the different "treasure island" pieces stuck on a board or a wall. Ask a volunteer from each team to go and try quickly to assemble the island. Time them.

2. Then read through the verse.

3. Have a pirate (a leader with a hat and patch on) sneak up and "steal" part of the treasure map while the children are saying it.

4. At the end of the verse, discover a piece is missing. Blame the children and carry on, asking the teams to repeat the verse back to you each time.

5. Allow the pirate to come creatively from different angles and continue to steal your treasure map, one piece at a time, until it all goes.

THEMED SNACK

Butterflies

You will need:

- Pineapple slices
- Cheese strings
- Glacé cherries
- Sprinkles
- Plastic knives
- Paper plates

1. Give each child a pineapple slice. They need to cut it in half; then turn the halves to make two curved butterfly wings.

2. Give each child half a cheese string, which they are to place in the middle of the pineapple wings as the butterfly's body.

3. Use a glacé cherry as the butterfly's head.

4. Decorate the wings with sprinkles.

5. As they are eating their snack, remind the children that a butterfly is often a picture of new life. Jesus beat death and offers us new life as his forgiven friends.

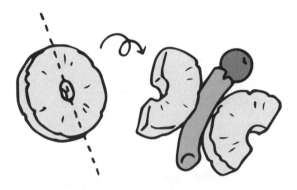

PRAYER SUGGESTION

When you pray with the children, it is good to explain that "amen" means "I agree", and that it gives them the option of joining in.

You will need:

- Lots of playdough

1. Give each child a lump of playdough, and ask them to roll it into a ball/stone shape.

2. As they are moulding their playdough, ask the children to think of one word to describe Jesus coming alive.

3. Ask them to tell you some of their words.

4. As the children hold the "stones" on their hands, say a prayer thanking God that Jesus came to die in our place, and to offer us forgiveness and everlasting life.

4-7s: Paper-plate tomb

You will need:
- Paper plates cut in half
- Grey or brown paper in small squares
- Grey or brown paper circle per child, for the rock
- Split pins
- Larger square of black paper, for the tomb entrance
- A sticker per child with Mark 16:6 printed on it: "He has risen! He is not here."

1. Ask the children to glue the black square in the middle of the plate.

2. Glue the squares of brown or grey paper around the rest of the plate, filling in the cave.

3. Help the children split pin the rock on one side of the tomb entrance, so it can either cover the entrance or be "rolled away".

4. Stick the Mark 16:6 label onto the black paper.

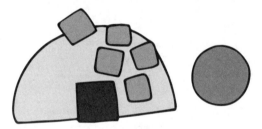

4-11s: Plant pots

You will need:
- Plant pots
- Compost
- Bulbs
- Paper – green and flower colours
- Pencil
- Scissors
- Green pipe cleaners (or straws)
- Sticky tape or glue
- Stapler

1. Fill the pot with sufficient compost so that bulbs placed on top can be covered with enough extra compost to bury them at the proper planting depth (at least 2cm/1 inch or more).

2. Put the bulb in and cover with more compost.

3. Trace a child's hand on paper. Cut the tracing out.

4. Curl each of the fingers around a pencil.

5. Using the palm of the handprint, form a cone (with the fingers curling outwards). Glue or tape the cone together to make a flower.

6. Staple the flower to a pipe cleaner or a drinking straw.

7. Draw some leaves on green paper, and then cut them out.

8. Staple or tape the leaves to the straw.

9. Make a few of these flowers for a beautiful bouquet that can be "planted" in the pot until the bulb grows.

4-11s: Easter gardens

You will need:
- *Müller-Corner* pots (yoghurt pot with a corner for fruit puree)
- Compost
- Funky-foam flowers
- Grass seeds
- Small, wrapped chocolate eggs, or pebbles
- Sticky tape
- Lollipop/popsicle sticks
- Raffia or twine
- Water

1. Fill the larger section of the pot with compost.

2. Sow the grass seed and lightly water.

3. Tilt the corner of the pot up, and stick the pebble or egg in front of it.

4. Decorate the outside of the pot with funky-foam flowers.

5. Make a wooden cross out of the lollipop/popsicle sticks and tie together by criss-crossing the raffia/twine.

6. Put the cross either in the far corner of the container or stick to the side, using tape.

8-11s: Comic strips

You will need:
- A copy of the comic-strip storyboard for each child (download from www.ceministries.org/epic)
- Felt-tip pens

1. Give each child a copy of the comic-strip storyboard.

2. Draw in the different stages of today's story, with speech bubbles and captions.

3. Encourage the children to think about who they could show their comic to, as a way of sharing the good news with other people.

Wiggle it!

You will need:
- An empty tissue box per team – these are the caves
- One belt per team
- Table-tennis balls x 5 per team – these are the stones

1. Ask for a volunteer from each team. Use the belts to tie a "cave" around their waists. Place five "stones" in each cave.

2. The volunteers have to jump up and down and wiggle and jiggle to get all the "stones" out of the "caves" as quickly as possible.

DRAMA

In today's drama, the three remaining Epic Explorers (Crop, Sonny and Berry) reach Crown Cave. Berry finds the riddle, and Sonny and Crop help her solve it. See page 148.

EPIC SCRATCH PAD
DISCUSSION GROUPS FOR 4-7s

Bible passage: Mark 16:1-8

Main aims

- Children will know that Jesus really did die and rise again.
- Children will understand that, because Jesus has beaten death, we can know life in him.

Introduction

- Welcome the children back.
- Learn the names of any new children.
- Remind them of your name.
- Recap on previous session, eg: "Last time, we saw that Jesus died in our place to take the punishment we deserve. He paid the price for our sin so we can be rescued. Jesus' death has made a way for us to be forgiven and accepted by God, and be friends with him for ever. We also saw some of the different ways that people reacted to Jesus' death."
- "This time we're going to think about Jesus rising from the dead. Did he really? And why does it matter?"

Booklet

If there's time and it's one of your chosen introductory activities, complete "Spot the difference" on page 22 of the *Scratch Pad*. (See page 108 of this Leader's Guide for how to run this activity.)

Photo findings

The recap below (called "Photo findings") appears on page 23 of the *Epic Scratch Pad*. It is a simple storyboard with the teaching summarized.

- Jesus definitely died.
- Then Jesus was alive!
- Jesus had promised these things.

As you look at the pictures, if you have time, you could ask the children to tell you if they remember what is happening.

Questions

Use the questions to encourage discussion.

1. Draw where Jesus' body was put after he died.

After the children have drawn the tomb and the stone, chat to them about how we know Jesus had definitely died.

- Pilate checked with the Roman centurion, who said it was true.
- Joseph of Arimathea then wrapped Jesus' body up like a mummy and buried it.
- And all this was witnessed by Mary and Mary.

However, not even death is stronger than Jesus.

2. What had moved when the women arrived at the tomb on Sunday?

The children have a choice of circling a tree, a stone or perfume.

When they have circled their answer, remind them that not only had the stone been moved, but the women also saw that Jesus was not there. An angel appeared to them and told them that Jesus had risen from the dead; that he was alive.

Explain that hundreds of people saw, touched and ate with Jesus. Jesus proved lots and lots of times that he is alive.

3. The woman shouldn't have been surprised that Jesus died and was then alive. It was all part of:

The children need to go over the lettering to reveal "God's rescue plan".

Explain that the women should have expected Jesus to be alive because Jesus had told them that it was going to happen.

4. Jesus is alive. How does that make you feel? Fill in this face...

Can you tell your leader why?

Ask the children to think about how they feel about Jesus coming back from the dead; and then get them to look up and show you that face. Once they have filled in the face outline in the booklet, ask them to tell you why, eg: "It makes me happy because I know that nothing is more powerful than Jesus", "It makes me confused because I don't understand how Jesus could do that", "It makes me surprised as I've never heard of anyone else coming back to life".

5. How important is it that Jesus died and is alive? Draw a stick man above your answer.

Explain that it is important that Jesus came alive because once again Jesus proves he is a promise-keeper as well as a promise-maker. We can trust his word. But more than that, because of his resurrection, we can know that God accepted Jesus' payment for our sin, and that death has been defeated as Jesus rose.

Jesus is now reigning in heaven and will one day return. He rules over everything, including life and death. Because our punishment has been taken,

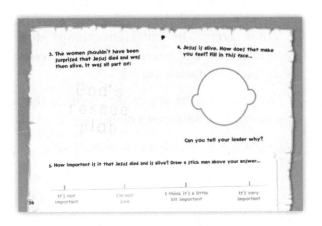

we can be forgiven and not separated from God, which means we can have new life too; we can live for ever with God.

If you have time, you may want to let the children do the puzzle on page 25, with some informal chat. If this is part of a holiday club or vacation Bible school, then the puzzle time is also a good opportunity to practise the memory verse and to plug any upcoming events or regular clubs.

Give out invitations to your family event.

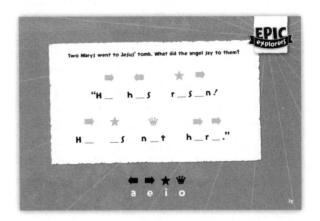

Conclusion

Finish by encouraging your group members to come back next time. Tell them: "We've seen why Jesus' resurrection matters to Christians. Next time, we're going to think about how we can know God's forgiveness and what it means to follow him."

Evaluate

- Is there anything you could add to your prayer cards? Was there anyone from the previous session missing today? You may be able to contact them and encourage them to come next time. If not, pray that they will return even without being contacted.

- Do you need to think about how to respond to any particular questions? Make sure you find time to plan your answer.

- Pray that the children will understand that, though they deserve punishment for their sin, God graciously offers them eternal life through Jesus.

(A downloadable version of these leader's notes for discussion groups is available from www.ceministries.org/epic.)

EPIC LOGBOOK
DISCUSSION GROUPS FOR 8-11s

Bible passage: Mark 16:1-8

Main aims
- Children will know that Jesus really did die and rise again.
- Children will understand that, because Jesus has beaten death, we can know life in him.

Introduction
- Welcome the children back.

- Recap on previous session, eg: "Last time, we saw that Jesus died in our place to take the punishment we deserve. He paid the price for our sin so we can be rescued. Jesus' death has made a way for us to be forgiven and accepted by God, and be friends with him for ever. We also saw some of the different ways that people reacted to Jesus' death."

- "This time we're going to think about Jesus rising from the dead. Did he really? And why does it matter?"

Booklet
If there's time and it's one of your chosen introductory activities, complete "Spot the difference" on page 22 of the *Logbook*. (See page 108 of this Leader's Guide for how to run this activity.)

Explorer's entries
The recap below (called "Explorer's entries") appears on page 23 of the *Epic Logbook*. If you have time, you may want to read through and summarize.

- Mark 15:42-47 – Jesus definitely died.
- Mark 16:1-8 – Jesus definitely rose again.
- In beating death, Jesus shows us that he is God and that we can have new life through him.

Questions
Use the questions to encourage discussion.

1. How do we know Jesus was definitely dead? (See Mark 15: 42-47.)

From Mark 15:42-47, we know that Jesus was definitely dead because Pilate checked with the Roman centurion, who confirmed it. Joseph of Arimathea was also convinced enough to take Jesus' body, wrap it and bury it – and all this was witnessed by Mary and Mary. However, not even death is stronger than Jesus.

2. What were the different things the women saw and heard when they arrived at the tomb (Mark 16: 4-6)?

Can you think of any other evidence that showed that Jesus was alive?

- They saw that the stone had been moved.
- They saw that Jesus was not there.
- They saw an angel and heard him say that Jesus had risen from the dead; that he was alive.

Explain that hundreds of people saw, touched and ate with Jesus. You may want to tell the children that many of Jesus' followers were put to death for insisting that he had risen from the dead. They wouldn't have been willing to die for something they weren't sure of.

3. Should the women have been surprised that Jesus rose from the dead? (Look at Mark 16:7 and then Mark 8:31.)

They shouldn't have been surprised, but rather, they should have expected it because Jesus had told them that it was going to happen.

4. Do you believe that Jesus died and came to life? Draw a stick man on the scale...

Let the children draw their stick man on the scale and then ask them to share their answers. Gently probe as to why they chose that point. You may need to go over the evidence once again or get them to think through alternatives if they say "no", eg:

- He fainted? But he had been tortured, crucified and stabbed through the heart with a spear by the Romans, who were expert killers!
- The body was stolen? Yet the tomb was guarded, a large stone covered it, a body was never found and he was seen by lots of witnesses.

5. Why is it important that Jesus rose again? Or isn't it?

It is important that Jesus rose again because once again Jesus proves he is a promise-keeper as well as a promise-maker. We can trust his word. But more than that, because of his resurrection, we can know that God accepted Jesus' payment for our sin, and that death has been defeated. Jesus is now reigning in heaven and will one day return. He rules over everything, including life and death.

And that's not all – as God gave Jesus new life, he also promises new life to those who believe Jesus died for them and who live his way. We deserve to be separated from God for ever, but Jesus rising from the dead shows us that God will give us life after we die; life for ever with him.

If you have time, you may want to let the children do the puzzles on page 25, with some informal chat. If this is part of a holiday club or vacation Bible school, then the puzzle time is also a good opportunity to practise the memory verse and to plug any upcoming events or regular clubs.

Conclusion

Finish by encouraging your group members to come back next time. Tell them: "We've seen why Jesus' resurrection matters to Christians. Next time, we're going to think about how we can know God's forgiveness and what it means to follow him."

Evaluate

- Is there anything you could add to your prayer cards? Was there anyone from the previous session missing today? You may be able to contact them and encourage them to come next time. If not, pray that they will return even without being contacted.

- Do you need to think about how to respond to any particular questions? Make sure you find time to plan your answer.

- Pray that the children will understand that, though they deserve punishment for their sin, God graciously offers them eternal life through Jesus.

(A downloadable version of these leader's notes for discussion groups is available from www.ceministries.org/epic.)

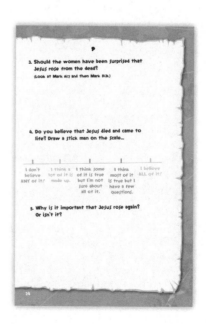

115

ROCKY ROAD
Following Jesus

Bible passage

Mark 8:27-38

Main aims

- Children will know that Jesus is God's Son and came to rescue us.
- Children will understand that following Jesus means putting him first even when it's tough.

Session options

The following pages include a wide variety of activities. See pages 14-19 for suggestions of which activities to choose for different contexts or length of time.

Notes for leaders

📖 *Read Mark 8:27-38*

"Follow my leader" is a popular game with younger children. The idea is that while someone is sent out of the room as "detective", a leader is chosen. The leader has to perform a certain action, and everyone else has to copy. For example, the leader may scratch their head or pull a face, and the rest of the group do the same. The "detective" returns to the room and has to try and work out who the leader is; they have to guess their identity.

Here in Mark 8, we begin with Jesus asking the question on his identity that has been posed throughout Mark: "Who am I?" (verses 27, 29). Peter's moment of recognition in verse 29 is as significant as that of the Roman centurion (Mark 15:39). And the answer that we give to the question is equally significant, as it will change our lives for ever. Following King Jesus as leader does not mean scratching our head or pulling a face, but rather, going through suffering before glory (verses 31-38).

Jesus puts his question of identity to his disciples in the town of Caesarea Philippi (verse 27), and they answer by sharing some of the different opinions people had (verse 28). As with some of the children in your group, despite all the disciples had seen, learned and heard, it's clear many of them were still confused about who Jesus was.

Peter, however, as he answers on behalf of the disciples, does see who Jesus is – he knows that Jesus is God's only chosen King, the Messiah/Christ (verse 29). Peter has had his eyes spiritually opened, but as the miracle immediately before illustrates (verses 22-26), it is only a partial understanding. Peter is yet to see the full implications of Jesus as the Messiah/Christ. He's yet to see Jesus as God (Mark 1:1, 11).

Fully aware of this, Jesus tells the disciples to keep quiet (verse 30). He then begins to teach them about the kind of King he actually is and why he came (verse 31). His revelation is mind-blowing!

Referring to himself as the "Son of Man" – a glorious, victorious figure (Daniel 7:13-14) – Jesus shares with his disciples how he will suffer and be rejected by religious rulers, and how he will be killed yet not destroyed, for he will rise again. He shares with them the certainty of these things happening.

Peter's blurred vision (verse 24) on what kind of King Jesus is leads to him trying to correct Jesus (verse 32). Peter does not realize that, without the cross, there can be no forgiveness or reconciliation; that, without death, there can be no resurrection. That is why Jesus is so quick to silence Peter (verse 33) – he knows that suffering cannot be avoided if he is to give his life as a ransom for many (Mark 10:45).

In verses 34-38, Jesus turns to the crowd and tells them that, if they are to follow him, they too must suffer. He calls for everyone to give up everything and follow obediently. It's important that the children grasp what this means – there is a cost to true discipleship. It will mean rejection and suffering; it will mean not living for self but for God; it will mean eternal gains. "He is no fool who gives up what he cannot keep, to gain what he cannot lose" (Jim Elliott, missionary, killed for his faith).

Leader's prayer: Pray that God will open the eyes of those in your group and that they will fully understand who Jesus is and why he came. Pray that they will see that the cost of following Jesus is totally worth it, and will want to seek him as Saviour and Lord.

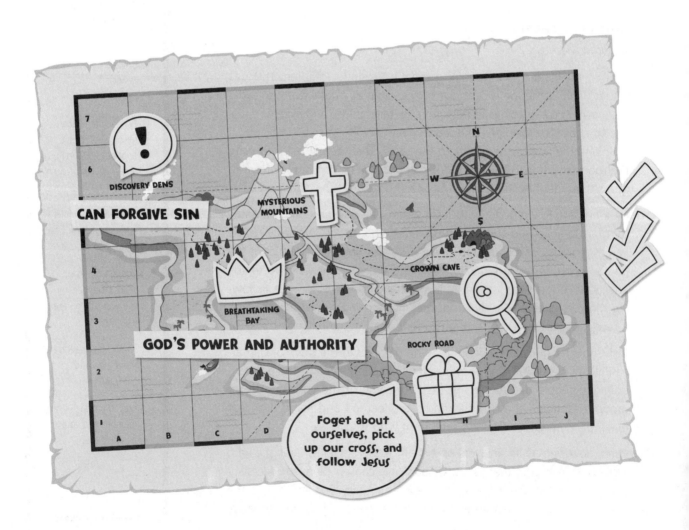

ROCKY ROAD:
TALK IDEA 1

Suitable for a holiday club or vacation Bible school, ages 4-11 or 8-11

You will need:

- Large-scale map of Adventure Island. (Gradually add the following visuals to the map through the talk, see page 118 - the visuals are on pages 154-155.)
- Coloured visuals of each location
- Labels with the following phrases:
  – "God's power and authority"
  – "Can forgive sin"
- Army camp with soldiers
- A large cross and 3 large ticks/check marks
- A speech bubble with: "Forget about ourselves, pick up our cross, and follow Jesus" written in it

This talk outline can also be downloaded from www.ceministries.org/epic

Children vote: Stop at different points during the story and ask children a question that has a "yes" or "no" answer. Ask them to show their answer by giving a "thumbs up" for "yes", and a "thumbs down" for "no".

What an amazing leader they had! For nearly three years, the disciples had followed Jesus and seen him do loads of incredible things. At Breathtaking Bay, we saw that the disciples had their breath taken away as they saw everyone stopping and listening when Jesus talked, because he spoke with authority. They saw him healing people with all sorts of illnesses.

> Add to the map: "Breathtaking Bay" coloured visual and, under the crown, the phrase: "God's power and authority"

In Discovery Dens, we discovered that the disciples saw how important forgiveness of sins is to Jesus.

> Add to the map: "Discovery Dens" coloured visual and, under the speech bubble, the phrase: "Can forgive sin".

Jesus had stopped storms and brought people back to life. It was no wonder everyone wanted to see him; he was the talk of every town.

So when Jesus asked them: "What are people saying? Who do people think I am?", do you think the disciples could answer? Vote now. (Children vote.)

Yes, they could. That day, as they walked to Caesarea Philippi, the disciples told Jesus that everyone was talking about him but no one could agree who he actually was. People thought he was some kind of special messenger from God.

But then Jesus asked his disciples a tougher question: "But what about you? Who do you say that I am?"

Well, they all had a ponder. Maybe they scratched their heads or twiddled their beards. Maybe they thought about some of the things they had seen and heard.

> Point to the map.

Eventually Peter spoke up: "I know! You're the Christ, the Messiah, the King promised and chosen by God!"

> Point to the crown on the "Breathtaking Bay" visual.

Who thinks Peter is right? (Children vote.)

Peter was right – kind of. You see, Peter knew Jesus was God's chosen King, but he didn't understand what kind of King. Peter probably thought that Jesus was going to be a warrior king, who would defeat the Romans and rule over everyone.

> Stick up the picture of the army camp on top of the mountains on the map.

But that wasn't the way God had planned to rescue his people.

Jesus wanted his disciples to know God's rescue plan, and so he told them exactly what would happen to him. He said that he would be treated badly by the religious leaders, and even be killed – but after three days he would rise again.

Stick up the "Mysterious Mountains" and "Crown Cave" coloured visuals (a cross and a magnifying glass).

Do you think the disciples believed that Jesus would be a different kind of King; a suffering King? Vote now. (Children vote.)

No way! "No Jesus, you're wrong!" Peter shouted. He didn't believe what he'd just heard. Jesus, the one who had done so many amazing things, the one who had shown such power, the one who had never done anything wrong? Surely he wouldn't suffer and die?

Hover a tick/check mark over the mountains and the cave.

Peter couldn't see how Jesus dying would bring rescue for his people – but was Jesus telling the truth? Vote now. (Children vote.)

Yes. Jesus always tells the truth.

Add the tick/check mark between the mountains and the cave.

We've seen in the last few days how Jesus suffered, died and rose again. It was all part of God's rescue plan for his Son, the promised King, to die in our place and deal with our sin problem. Jesus knew he had to take our punishment to make it possible for us to be forgiven and become friends with God for ever.

I wonder, do you believe that? Do you believe that Jesus is God's Son and the promised King, who can forgive us? Have a think in your heads.

Add a tick/check mark to both the crown and the speech bubble (with an exclamation mark in it). Then point at the cross by Mysterious Mountains.

Do you believe Jesus died and rose again to rescue us?

I want you to vote – but this time just quietly in your heads. (Children vote.)

So, how can we receive this gift of forgiveness and be friends with God? Well, just after Jesus told Peter and the others about God's rescue plan, he explained to them what it means to be his follower.

Point at the Rocky Road on the map; then stick on the "Rocky Road" coloured visual (a gift).

Jesus said that we must "forget about ourselves, pick up our cross, and follow him".

Stick speech bubble on by the gift.

"Forget about ourselves" means that we should want to please Jesus and live God's way, not just please ourselves. We should say sorry for the times we're selfish, for the times we say, think and do wrong.

"Pick up our cross" means that we are prepared to go through difficult times just because we love God. We may be teased or ignored, or people may even try to make us give up living God's way.

"Follow" means that we are thankful that Jesus died in our place, and we want to copy the way Jesus lived and loved. We choose to obey him as the King, even when we don't feel like it, because he has done so much for us.

God promises to forgive us and help us live his way, if we believe Jesus is his Son and the promised King, who died to rescue us. I wonder, are you ready to follow Jesus?

Vote one last time, again in your head. (Children vote.)

If you voted "yes", then make sure you chat to your group leader about it. They'll talk to you a little more about what it means to be a follower of Jesus.

ROCKY ROAD: TALK IDEA 2

Suitable for a mid-week club or children's Christianity Explored course, ages 8-11

You will need:
- The visual from week 1 (see page 58)
- A flip-chart pad on a stand, prepared in advance as shown on page 122
- The Explorer Notebook (see page 156)
- Marker pen
- 10 laminated crosses (see page 155) and Blu-tack reuseable adhesive
- A wrapped-up gift with something small in it, eg: a packet of sweets/candies

This talk outline can also be downloaded from www.ceministries.org/epic

Show page 1 of the flip chart.

What are you like when it comes to making choices? I wonder would you rather:

• Always lose?
• Never play?

Have the children vote by making an "X" with their arms to show their choice; then ask one volunteer to come up and stick a cross in the check box voted for by the majority.

Repeat with a couple of other choices on pages 2 and 3.

We make choices all the time. Just think about all the choices you've made even today. What to have for your breakfast... Whether you'll listen to your mum...

I wonder how important your choices were. Do you think they will affect you tomorrow? And the next day? And the day after that?

Well, since some of us are just starting to explore what the Bible says about Jesus, we're going to look at a true story from before Jesus died.

It's when Jesus' first followers had to make a choice about who they thought Jesus was

and what he came to do. It was an important choice and one that would affect them every single day. And it's one that helps us see what it means to be a Christian – to be someone who follows Jesus.**

1. A Christian is someone who understands who Jesus is

In Mark 8, we're told that Jesus' followers were walking along a road with Jesus, when all of a sudden he asked them who they thought he was. Which answer do you think they chose?

Show page 4 of the flip-chart pad. Ask someone to come and stick a cross in the check box by the option they personally think the disciples said.

• Read Mark 8:29b

How did Peter describe Jesus? (Take answers)

That's right, Peter said that Jesus is the Messiah/Christ.

Note: "Messiah", in Hebrew, and "Christ", in Greek, are the same title. Choose whichever one is used in the Bible version you are looking at in the discussion groups.

Can I have a volunteer to come up and cross out all the "X's" in the puzzle to help us see what it means?

When the volunteer crosses out all of the "X's", ask them to read out what it now says: "God's promised chosen King".

Peter was right, but Jesus wasn't just God's chosen King; he was also God's Son (show page 1 of the Explorer Notebook). **Time and again in Mark, we've seen Jesus showing authority that only God has. That's why he was able to teach powerfully, heal people, forgive sins and beat death.**

Point to week 1's visual.

A Christian is someone who believes Jesus is God's Son.

Prepare the following flip-chart sheets if you are using talk idea 2.

1
☐ **Always lose**
☐ **Never play**

2
☐ **Be born with an elephant trunk**
☐ **Be born with a giraffe neck**

3
☐ **Accept a gift**
☐ **Reject a gift**

4
*(depending on Bible version)

A Christian understands who Jesus is

☐ **A kind man**
☐ **A good teacher**
☐ **A messenger from God**
☐ **The Messiah/ The Christ***
☐ **God's Son**

XGXOXDS PXROXMXIXSXED
CXHXOXSXEXN KXIXNXG

5
A Christian understands why Jesus died and rose again

6
A Christian is someone who follows Jesus

ME ME ME

7
A Christian is someone who says "yes" to Jesus' free gift

☐ **Keep finding out more by coming along to**

_____
(fill in the name of your weekly children's group)

☐ **Ask a leader some more questions to help you understand**
☐ **Leave it for now**
☐ **Ready to "ABCD"**

2. A Christian is someone who understands why Jesus died and rose again

Just after Peter has realized who Jesus is, Jesus tells his followers that they can't let anyone else know. And then he explains why.

- **Read Mark 8:31**

Jesus told his followers that he was going to be killed, but would rise to life on the third day.

Show page 5 of the flip chart, and, as you're explaining about Jesus predicting his death, stick three crosses onto the mound.

Peter was so shocked to hear that Jesus would die that he told him off! He probably thought that Jesus, as God's chosen King, was going to rescue them from the Romans. But that wasn't the kind of rescue Jesus had come for.

Jesus silenced Peter because he knew he must die; he had to die. We've seen in the last two sessions* that Jesus died and rose again because it was the only way he could solve our sin problem (show page 2 of the Explorer Notebook) **and rescue us from the punishment we deserve** (turn to page 3 of the Explorer Notebook, and then page 4).

Do you believe that, through Jesus' death, we can be forgiven and be brought back into friendship with God?

*If you combined sessions 3 and 4, say: "last session" here.

3. A Christian is someone who follows Jesus

But listen – a Christian isn't just someone who understands who Jesus is and why he came. A Christian is also someone who wants to do things God's way – not their own.

- **Read Mark 8:34**

Turn to page 6 of the flip-chart pad.

The verse says we should deny ourselves. That means we no longer make our choices just on what *we* want to do, and we no longer think we matter more than other people or God.

Put a cross over the words "Me, me, me".

Instead, we should want to please Jesus and live God's way – whether it's how we speak to our parents, how we treat our friends or how we spend our time. And it means we say sorry for the times we're selfish, and for the times we say, think and do wrong.

But the verse mentioned a cross – a symbol of suffering. It may be that people tease or ignore us, and even try to make us give up living as a Christian. But if we follow Jesus, we should be prepared to go through difficult times just because we love God. Jesus called it "taking up our cross".

Stick a cross on the body of the stick man.

Jesus also said: "Follow me". A Christian is someone who is thankful that Jesus died in our place and therefore wants to copy the way Jesus lived and loved.

Draw an arrow upwards from the stick man, and then a crown above the arrowhead.

A Christian is someone who chooses to follow and obey Jesus as the King, even when they don't feel like it.

"Deny, suffer and obey"! You might be thinking: "That sounds hard. Why bother?" Well, Jesus warned us that if people choose to reject him, then he will reject us. But if we follow Jesus, he will save us. Jesus promises that he will help us live his way. And he promises that if we are forgiven by him, we will live with him for ever.

Show page 5 of the Explorer Notebook.

So a Christian is:

- Someone who understands that Jesus is God's Son.
- Someone who understands that Jesus died to take our punishment.
- Someone who follows Jesus and lives his way.

4. A Christian is someone who says "yes" to a free gift from Jesus

But there's one more thing that a Christian is…

A Christian is someone who says "yes" to a free gift from Jesus. I have an amazing gift here that I want to give away.

Hold up wrapped gift.

Would you like my free gift?

Offer the gift to a child – let them take it and open it.

All you had to do for that gift to be yours was accept it from me. You didn't need to do anything else.

Jesus offers us the free gift of forgiveness and forever friendship with him. We don't have to do anything for it; we just need to accept what Jesus did on the cross to rescue us. The way you can do that is to:

- ADMIT your sin. Tell God that you are sorry that you don't treat him as you should. Ask him to forgive you.

- BELIEVE that Jesus died to take the punishment you deserve, and that he rose to life, and he is alive today.

- CONSIDER the cost of living as Jesus' follower from now on, with him in charge. Remember what we've just learned – it won't always be easy putting God first. Ask him to help you.

- DO something about it! Will you choose to accept Jesus' free gift and choose to live in a way that pleases him from now on?

I wonder, at the end of this course/club, what choice will you make?

Show page 7 of flip-chart pad and as you talk through the options, hover a cross over each tick/check box:

☐ **Keep finding out more by coming along to _____** (fill in the name of your weekly children's group)

☐ **Ask a leader some more questions to help you understand**

☐ **Leave it for now**

☐ **Ready to "ABCD". Let a leader know if that's you!**

Ideas menu

INTRODUCTORY ACTIVITIES

Choose at least one of the following activities, to suit your group, your context and the time you have available. Most of the games can be adapted to work from the front or in a small-group setting.

Who am I?

Aim: To help the children begin to see that the more clues we have, the easier it is to identify someone.

You will need a blindfold.

1. Choose a child to be blindfolded, and ask them to sit on a chair at the front.

2. Choose another person to stand in front of the chair. The child on the chair has three guesses to see if he can guess who it is.

3. Before the first guess, the only clue he has is the sound of the person walking up to him.

4. Before the second guess, the blindfolded child can stand up and touch the person's face.

5. Before the third guess, the blindfolded child can ask the other person to say just one word.

6. Repeat, if you have time.

At the end, explain that the more clues you had, the easier it was to recognize the other person. Today we're going to see Jesus asking his disciples to think about all the clues they've had, and see if they can recognize who he is.

Follow the leader

Aim: To introduce the idea of what it means to copy and follow the one who is in charge.

1. Ask everyone to stand in a circle, facing inwards.

2. Ask one person to leave – they will be the guesser for the round.

3. Decide upon a leader. They will then start doing an action everyone copies.

4. Call the guesser back in.

5. The leader should keep changing moves regularly (eg: marching, clapping, jumping, etc.), and everyone else should copy, but trying not to be too obvious who the leader is.

6. The guesser must keep moving round to try and spot the leader. They are allowed up to three guesses.

7. Repeat.

Afterwards, explain that today we're going to see that Jesus calls us to follow him. That means having him as our leader, copying his actions and obeying his ways. Everyone should be able to see that we're following Jesus.

Follow my leader obstacle course

Aim: To learn what it means to follow and that it's not always easy.

You will need some blindfolds and some objects to use as obstacles, eg: beanbags, cones.

1. Before the session, design a simple obstacle course.

2. Ask the children to get into pairs. One is to be blindfolded while the other is to lead them around the obstacle course. It may be a good idea to match younger children with older children, if you have a mixed age-group.

At the end, explain that following Jesus isn't always easy – just as following their leader wasn't easy. But Jesus will never leave us and longs to help us.

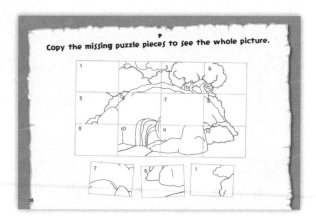

Jigsaw

Aim: To see that, when all the pieces are put together, we see the whole picture.

You will need the *Epic Scratch Pads* and/or *Logbooks*.

1. On page 28 of the booklets, there is a picture with some pieces missing. The spare pieces are around the side.

2. The children are to work out which piece goes where; then copy those pieces to complete the picture. (With younger children you may prefer to ask them to draw an arrow showing where each piece goes, rather than copying it.)

3. You could also bring in some simple jigsaws for the children to complete.

Afterwards, explain that once all the pieces were put together, we could see the whole picture. Today we're going to put together the pieces from the last few sessions and we'll see a picture of God's rescue plan.

MEMORY VERSE

Ping pong

1. Call up a child each from two teams who thinks they know the verse. Have them stand back to back.

2. Have the first child call out the first word of the verse and the other child say the next – and then back and forth until someone makes a mistake or forgets.

3. The one who messed up goes and sits down while everyone says the verse.

4. Call up another contender (from a third team, if you have more than two) to go up against the "ping-pong champion".

THEMED SNACK

What am I?

You will need:
- Plates
- Assortment of small snacks, eg: popcorn, Cheerios, grapes (not nuts, in case any child has a nut allergy)
- Blindfolds
- Pieces of (nut-free) Rocky Road bars

1. Before serving snacks, ask the children to cover their eyes or put on a blindfold.

2. Serve them one thing each, and let them guess what they are eating.

3. Afterwards give them a Rocky Road to munch on, since it's the name of the session and a treat for the last time you meet.

Chat about the fact that Jesus asked his friends to identify him. Even though they had seen him do lots of amazing things, they still couldn't see clearly. Jesus is God's Son and the promised King.

PRAYER SUGGESTION

When you pray with the children, it is good to explain that "amen" means "I agree", and that it gives them the option of joining in.

1. Ask the children to point upwards. Pray: "Thank you for sending Jesus your Son as our promised King".

2. Ask the children to put a finger from one hand on the palm of the other hand, and then swap hands. Pray: "Thank you that Jesus died to pay for our sin".

3. Ask the children to cross hands over their chest, saying: "Thank you that your love for us is so great".

4. Ask the children to "walk" two fingers on the palm of their other hand. Pray: "Please help us understand what it means to follow you".

5. Ask the children to thump their fist into the palm of their other hand. Pray: "Please help us to live your way even when it's tough".

CRAFT IDEAS

4-7s: Finger puppets

You will need:
- A finger puppet outline* per person on card (card stock), see page 158
- Felt-tip pens
- Scissors

* This needs to be a blank template so the children can decorate it as if it is themselves.

1. Ask the children to cut out the person and the finger holes (they may need help with this).

2. Colour in and decorate the puppet, making it look like themselves.

3. Put their fingers through and walk along the table top.

Remind the children that they need to choose if they want to follow Jesus.

4-11s: Group banners

You will need:
- Large sheets of paper, with outline letters spelling "Son of God" in the middle of a crown
- Shiny paper
- Stickers
- Glue
- Glitter
- Bamboo canes
- Sticky tape
- Gold or silver paint
- Paint brushes
- Water pots
- Felt-tip pens

1. Remind the children that Jesus is God's Son and our King, who died for us and wants us to follow him. Tell them that we are going to make a banner to help us to remember that.

2. Ask the children to use the shiny paper and glitter to fill in the letters.

3. Then paint the crown.

4. Next, tell the children to write words to describe Jesus around the outside of the crown, and add on the stickers.

5. Stick a cane to the top of the banner and display.

4-11s: Door hangers

You will need:
- Door hanger template (see page 128) photocopied on card (card stock)
- PVA (white) glue
- Glue spreaders
- Scissors
- Funky-foam sheets and letters
- Stickers
- Mark 8:34 printed on labels in an outline font

1. Ask the children to cut out a cross from funky foam and glue it to the door-hanger template.

2. Underneath stick on the Bible verse.

3. The children can use funky-foam letters and other items to decorate the other side of the door hanger, as well as colouring in the Bible verse.

4. Encourage them to hang the door hanger up at home as a reminder that we should "take up our cross". Check that they remember what it means to "take up their cross".

8-11s: Funky footwear

You will need:
- Thin card (card stock)
- Scissors
- Paint
- Brushes
- Water pots
- Beads
- Pipe cleaners
- PVA (white) glue
- Pens
- Duct tape

1. Have the children draw around their shoe on the card (card stock).

2. Cut out the shoe outline.

3. Poke a hole where the toe grip on the shoe would be; and two more, halfway down on either side.

4. Place two pipe cleaners through the front hole and fold over on the underside. Stick down with duct tape.

5. Paint the card outline.

6. Thread beads onto the pipe cleaners.

7. Thread the end of the pipe cleaners through the side holes and stick down on the underside.

8. Remind the children that Jesus calls us to follow him.

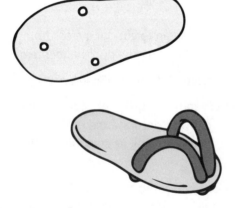

Snake race

You will need:
- One sleeping bag per team

1. Have one volunteer from each team climb into a sleeping bag.

2. They then have to race down the rocky road to the finish line by sliding in the sleeping bags on their stomachs.

DRAMA

In the closing drama, the children walk along Rocky Road. Sonny chooses to stop, but Berry and Crop continue to explore. See page 148.

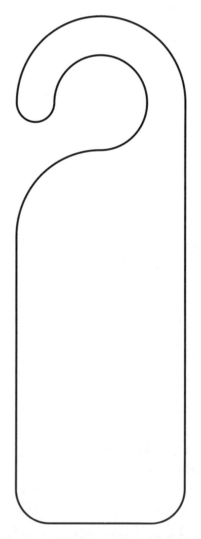

Photocopy at 200% to make a template for the Door Hanger craft (page 127), or download at full size from www.ceministries.org/epic

EPIC SCRATCH PAD
DISCUSSION GROUPS FOR 4-7s

Bible passage: Mark 8:27-38

Main aims

- Children will know that Jesus is God's Son and came to rescue us.
- Children will understand that following Jesus means putting him first even when it's tough.

Introduction

- Welcome the children back.

- Learn the names of any new children.

- Remind them of your name.

- Recap on previous session, eg: "Last time we saw that Jesus didn't stay dead. He died on a Friday, but rose to life on the Sunday. Jesus had said he would come to life – and he did! This shows that Jesus' words always come true, and also that God accepted the price Jesus paid for our sin. Jesus is still alive today, reigning as King in heaven. One day he will return again."

- "This time we're going to think about God's rescue plan, and what it means to follow Jesus."

Booklet

If there's time and it's one of your chosen introductory activities, complete "Jigsaw" on page 28 of the *Scratch Pad*. (See page 126 of this Leader's Guide for how to run this activity.)

Photo findings

The recap below (called "Photo findings") appears on page 29 of the *Epic Scratch Pad*. It is a simple storyboard with the teaching summarized.

- Jesus is God's Son. He is King of everything.
- Jesus had to die to take our punishment.
- Following Jesus is hard but worth it!

As you look at the pictures, if you have time, you could ask the children to tell you if they remember what is happening.

Questions

Use the questions on pages 29 and 30 to encourage discussion.

1. Jesus asked: "Who am I?" Peter thought Jesus was the...

Once the children fill in "king" and draw a crown, ask them if they can remember different ways in which we've seen that Jesus is God's Son and the promised King. Explain that, like the disciples, the more time we spend looking at Jesus, the more evidence we will see showing us who he is and why he came.

2. Who do you think Jesus is?

☐ **Jesus is a good, kind man**

☐ **Jesus was a special teacher**

☐ **Jesus is a made-up person**

☐ **Jesus is God's Son and King**

☐ **Someone else**

How the children answer will give you insight into how their thinking has developed over the sessions. You may even want to point that out to them.

3. What did Jesus have to do so that we can be forgiven? Draw it below...

As they are drawing the cross, say that Jesus paid for our sins by dying on the cross.

After they have finished, explain that the Bible tells us that God accepts us, not because of anything *we* have done, but because of what *Jesus* has done. God's perfect Son died on the cross in our place.

4. Jesus died and came to life so that we can be his forgiven friends. We need to...

The children need to cross out the "X's" to spell "TURN" and "SORRY".

It's a bit like accepting an invitation. Jesus says that if we follow him, we will suffer too – but he promises to help us.

When we have seen how much God has done for us, and how he longs for the best for us, we should want to turn from living *our* way to living *his* way. We need to realize that we have done wrong and we desperately need his rescue. We need to say sorry, and ask for his forgiveness and free gift of eternal life.

You could illustrate this by standing facing the wall, with your arms folded – and point out this is like when we ignore and disobey God. Then turn around and march on the spot. Explain this is like when we turn around and want to start listening to God and following his ways.

Offer a sweet to someone. Ask what they have to do to make it their own. They have to take it – it's no good just looking at it or knowing about it; they need to accept it and make it their own.

Go though ways of accepting Jesus' invitation to be his friend, and how we can start living with Jesus as our rescuing King:

1. Say "sorry" to God for not treating him as you should.

2. Say "thank you" to God for sending Jesus to die so that you can be forgiven.

3. Ask God to please forgive you, and help you to turn and live his way.

Ask the children to let you know at the end if they would like to find out more about following Jesus and becoming God's friend.

5.   Do you have any questions about what it means to follow Jesus?

Use this as a time to answer any unanswered questions. If there are children in your group who are already Christians, you may want to ask them to share what it's like for them to follow Jesus.

If you have time, you may want to let the children do the puzzles on page 31, with some informal chat. If this is part of a holiday club or vacation Bible school, then the puzzle time is also a good opportunity to practise the memory verse and to plug any upcoming events or regular clubs.

Give out invitations to your family event.

Conclusion

Finish by thanking the children for coming along and encourage them to keep attending groups run by your church.

Depending on where you feel the majority of your group are spiritually, and your understanding of their parents, you may want to encourage them to respond to what they've learned and put their trust in Jesus.

They may want to do this now, in which case you can remind them what it means to "ABCD" (if you included this in the talk), or to pray "sorry, thank you, please". Give the child an opportunity to say their own prayer asking God to forgive them, thanking him for sending Jesus, and asking him to help them live as a follower of Jesus from now on. Or they may prefer to talk to someone about this away from the group later – you, another leader or their parents.

Alternatively you may want to pray a more general prayer with the group, eg:

> *Dear God, thank you so much for the Bible and all we've been able to look at in Mark's Gospel. Thank you that you want us to understand who Jesus is and why he came. I still have so many questions, so please will you help me to discover the answers, and help me see how much you love me. Amen.*

You may want to give the children a gospel tract, eg: "Who will be King?" or "Why did Jesus die?" (available from The Good Book Company websites), and encourage them to read it through with their parents. This helps to avoid parents feeling as if they are being alienated or that their children are being pressurized. It also gives the parents an opportunity to think through the gospel for themselves!

Evaluate

• Is there anything you could add to your prayer cards? Keep these safe and keep praying for the children that have been in your group.

• Do any of the children need information on regular groups run by the church? Make sure you send them the details this week.

• Praise God for all of the children in your group and the privilege it has been to share the good news of Jesus with them.

• Pray for those who are not yet Christians – ask that they will be convicted of their need to accept God's gift of forgiveness.

• Pray for those who are followers of Jesus, that they will grow in grace and understanding, and that they will be bold in telling their friends about Jesus.

(A downloadable version of these leader's notes for discussion groups is available from www.ceministries.org/epic.)

EPIC LOGBOOK
DISCUSSION GROUPS FOR 8-11s

Bible passage: Mark 8:27-38

Main aims

- Children will know that Jesus is God's Son and came to rescue us.
- Children will understand that following Jesus means putting him first even when it's tough.

Introduction

- Welcome the children back.
- Learn the names of any new children.
- Remind them of your name.
- Recap on previous session, eg: "Last time we saw that Jesus didn't stay dead. He died on a Friday, but rose to life on the Sunday. Jesus had said he would come to life – and he did! This shows that Jesus' words always come true, and also that God accepted the price Jesus paid for our sin. Jesus is still alive today, reigning as King in heaven. One day he will return again."
- "This time we're going to think about God's rescue plan, and what it means to follow Jesus."

Booklet

If there's time and it's one of your chosen introductory activities, complete "Jigsaw" on page 28 of the *Logbook*. (See page 126 of this Leader's Guide for how to run this activity.)

Explorer's entries

The recap below (called "Explorer's entries") appears on page 29 of the *Epic Logbook*. If you have time, you may want to read through and summarize.

- Mark 8:29 – Jesus is God's Son. He is King over everything.
- Mark 8:31 – Jesus had to die to provide the way for us to be forgiven.
- Mark 8:34 – If we love God, we should want to live his way even if it's hard.

Questions

Use the questions to encourage discussion.

1. What answer would you have given to Jesus' question: "Who am I?"

How the children answer will give you insight into how their thinking has developed over the sessions. You may even want to point that out to them. Explain that like the disciples, the more time we spend looking at Jesus, the more evidence we will see showing us who he is and why he came.

2. Which of these do you believe?

- ☐ **I am a good person and hope I deserve to go to heaven.**
- ☐ **God will let me into heaven because I'm not that bad.**
- ☐ **I don't deserve it, but I can go to heaven because Jesus died to rescue me from my sin.**
- ☐ **I have done wrong and deserve to be punished by God.**

This question should highlight any misconceptions there still are regarding their salvation. The children may tick more than one box. After they have shared their answers, chat with them about the fact that the Bible teaches us that none of us deserve to go to heaven and none of us can earn our way there, no matter how we behave. However, consider with them the fact that even though we don't deserve it, God longs for us to be in his family, to be forgiven by him.

3. How does the Bible say we can be accepted and forgiven by God?

The Bible tells us that God accepts us, not because of anything *we* have done, but because of what *Jesus* has done. God's perfect Son died on the cross in our place. We need to realize that we have done wrong and we desperately need his rescue. We need to ask for his forgiveness and the free gift of eternal life.

Offer a sweet/candy to someone. Ask what they have to do to make it their own.

They have to take it – it's no good just looking at it or knowing about it; they need to accept it and make it their own.

When we have seen how much God has done for us and how he longs for the best for us, we should want to turn from living *our* way, to living *his* way.

You could illustrate this by standing facing the wall, with your arms folded – and point out this is like when we ignore and disobey God. Then turn around and march on the spot. Explain this is like when we turn around and want to start listening to God and following his ways.

Go through ways of accepting Jesus' invitation to be his friend, and how we can start living with Jesus as our rescuing King. If you had the talk with the "ABCD" illustration in, you may want to recap on that:

- ADMIT your sin. Tell God that you are sorry that you don't treat him as you should. Ask him to forgive you.

- BELIEVE that Jesus died to take the punishment you deserve; that he came to life; and that he is alive today.

- CONSIDER the cost of living as Jesus' follower from now on, with him in charge. Remember what we saw earlier – it won't always be easy putting him first. Ask God to help you.

- DO something about it! Will you choose to accept Jesus' free gift and to live in a way that pleases him from now on?

Alternatively you may want to simply explain that we can:

1. Say "sorry" to God for not treating him as we should.

2. Say "thank you" to God for sending Jesus to die so that we can be forgiven.

3. Ask God to please forgive us, and help us to turn and live his way.

Ask the children to let you know at the end if they would like to find out more about following Jesus and becoming God's friend. There are some suggestions in the conclusion about what you should do if a child does speak about becoming a Christian.

4. "Being a Christian is just not worth it. You end up having no fun and having no friends. What's the point?" Which bit of this statement seems true? Why do you want/not want to follow Jesus?

This will help unpack the cost of being a Christian, as for many children that will be a new idea. Help consider with them that sometimes it can be difficult to live God's way – it may mean saying "no" to some things and being teased; at other times, it may be harder still. However, if we are Christians, then we are not on our own. We have God with us now, longing to help us and change us, and we have the promise of living with him for ever when we die.

If the children say that they need more time, encourage them to keep coming along to your church groups and to keep exploring.

5. Do you have any questions about what it means to follow Jesus?

Use this as a time to answer any unanswered questions. If there are children in your group who are already Christians, you may want to ask them to share what it's like for them to follow Jesus.

If you have time, you may want to let the children do the puzzles on page 31, with some informal chat. If this is part of a holiday club or vacation Bible school, then the puzzle time is also a good opportunity to practise the memory verse and to plug any upcoming events or regular clubs.

Give out invitations to your family event.

Conclusion

Finish by thanking the children for coming along and encourage them to keep attending groups run by your church.

Depending on where you feel the majority of your group are spiritually, and your understanding of their parents, you may want to encourage them to respond to what they've learned and put their trust in Jesus.

They may want to do this now, in which case you can remind them what it means to "ABCD", or to pray "sorry, thank you, please" (page 132). Give the child an opportunity to say their own prayer asking God to forgive them, thanking him for sending Jesus, and asking him to help them live as a follower of Jesus from now on. Or they may prefer to talk to someone about this away from the group later – you, another leader or their parents.

Alternatively you may want to pray a more general prayer with the group, eg:

Dear God, thank you so much for the Bible and all we've been able to look at in Mark's Gospel. Thank you that you want us to understand who Jesus is and why he came. I still have so many questions, so please will you help me to discover the answers, and help me see how much you love me. Amen.

You may want to give the children a gospel tract, eg: "Who will be King?" or "Why did Jesus die?" (available from The Good Book Company websites), and encourage them to read it through with their parents. This helps to avoid parents feeling as if they are being alienated or that their children are being pressurized. It also gives the parents an opportunity to think through the gospel for themselves!

Evaluate

- Is there anything you could add to your prayer cards? Keep these safe and keep praying for the children that have been in your group.

- Do any of the children need information on regular groups run by the church? Make sure you send them the details this week.

- Praise God for all of the children in your group and the privilege it has been to share the good news of Jesus with them.

- Pray for those who are not yet Christians – ask that they will be convicted of their need to accept God's gift of forgiveness.

- Pray for those who are followers of Jesus, that they will grow in grace and understanding, and that they will be bold in telling their friends about Jesus.

(A downloadable version of these leader's notes for discussion groups is available from www.ceministries.org/epic.)

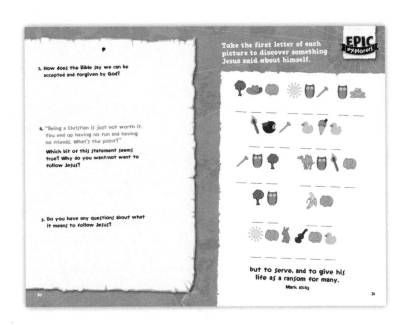

FAMILY EVENTS
Family Service

This family service is ideal to use on the Sunday at the end of an *Epic Explorers* Bible club or vacation Bible school.

If you keep the elements moving quickly, the service will take one hour.

Main aims

■ To give adults a flavour of the week, including sharing what has been taught.

■ To encourage parents to think about attending a Christianity Explored course.

Time	Activity		Leader
	Tick when materials are ready for each section	✔	
2 minutes	Welcome		
3 minutes	Song		
2 minutes	A short introduction to the week and the service		
3 minutes	Children sing the theme song		
5 minutes	Talk 1: Who is Jesus? Jesus is God's Son. He is King of everything (page 136).		
3 minutes	Another song from the week		
4 minutes	Memory verse: have children up at the front saying the verse Invite children to come to the regular children's groups		
3 minutes	Another song from the week		
8 minutes	Talk 2: Why did Jesus come? Jesus can forgive sins. He died to make that possible (page 137).		
3 minutes	Another song from the week		
7 minutes	Quiz – based on the week's teaching, but also have questions for the adults		
5 minutes	Either a summary of the drama or a slideshow/video of the week		
3 minutes	Song		
6 minutes	Talk 3: What does it mean to follow Jesus? Jesus rose to show our sins can be forgiven. We need to choose if we will follow him (page 138).		
3 minutes	Final points and theme song		

Have prize giving and refreshments / meal / barbeque after the service.

SUMMARY TALK FOR FAMILY SERVICE

Suitable for an all-age service at the end of a holiday club or vacation Bible school

Note: This summary is divided into three short talks. See page 135 to see how they fit within the plan for the whole service.

For the three talks you will need:
- The giant map of the island, with five labels stuck on the 5 related locations: Mark 1, Mark 2, Mark 15, Mark 16, Mark 8.
- The coloured visuals for each location
- Five extra labels to add to the map:
  - "Son" for Breathtaking Bay
  - "Forgiver" for Discovery Dens
  - "Died" for Mysterious Mountains
  - "Rose" for Crown Cave
  - "Follow?" for Rocky Road

This talk outline can also be downloaded from www.ceministries.org/epic

TALK 1: WHO IS JESUS?

(Jesus is God's Son. He is the King of everything.)

Do you like exploring? Checking out new places? Discovering new things? We've been on an epic adventure this week as we've explored true stories from the Bible about Jesus. We started in Mark 1:

Stick up "Breathtaking Bay" visual.

At "Breathtaking Bay" we began to discover evidence that Jesus is God's Son, and the King of everything, just as Mark claimed at the beginning of his book.

Have up on the screen Mark 1:1.
"The beginning of the good news about Jesus the Messiah, the Son of God."

I wonder what you'd be like if someone walked into your workplace or school tomorrow and told you to get up and leave immediately. That's what happened to two brothers called Simon and Andrew.

Some of you may be thinking: "That'd be great!" But what if that person then asked

to you leave absolutely everything – not just your work, but your homes, your families, the lot. Are you so keen now? I thought not. We would probably just ignore them or think they were joking. And yet, at Breathtaking Bay, we read this...

"As Jesus walked beside the Sea of Galilee, he saw Simon and his brother Andrew casting a net into the lake, for they were fishermen. "Come, follow me," Jesus said, "and I will send you out to fish for people." At once they left their nets and followed him. When he had gone a little farther, he saw James son of Zebedee and his brother John in a boat, preparing their nets. Without delay he called them, and they left their father Zebedee in the boat with the hired men and followed him." (Mark 1:16-20)

Show pictures of the story while the passage is read – available to download from www.ceministries.org/epic

When Jesus told the fishermen to leave everything, they obeyed. Immediately. No delaying, arguing and ignoring. They upped and left because they knew he had the authority to say this. They knew if Jesus commanded them to follow, they had to follow.

Can you imagine having such authority when you speak? "Tidy up" and it happens immediately; "Be quiet" and instantly the arguing stops; "Give me chocolate" and they do; "Buy me" and it's in your hand as quick as a flash. But these things don't happen. Our words are not powerful like Jesus' words were. He spoke, and right away things happened.

And it wasn't just when he told people to follow him. As we continued on our expedition in Mark 1, we had our breath taken away time and again.

- Jesus spoke – and evil spirits fled.
- Jesus spoke – and people were healed.
- Jesus spoke – and the crowds were amazed.

How could he do all these things? The amazing claim is that Jesus has such power over everything and everyone because he is the one who fuels the sun and drives the rotation of the planets. He is the one who created and controls all things.

When the explorer Christopher Columbus arrived in the Bahamas, he called the locals "Indians" because he was convinced he was in Asia. He had mistaken their identity. But there's no mistaken identity in Mark 1. At Breathtaking Bay, we saw that Jesus is God's King and Son.

Add "Son" to the map under the crown on "Breathtaking Bay".

And at Breathtaking Bay we had a glimpse of a land far greater than has ever been explored; of a kingdom where there will be no suffering, fear or death; of a place where Jesus will reign as King.

The other stories we looked at showed us how we can be in that kingdom. More about that later...

TALK 2: WHY DID JESUS COME?

(Jesus can forgive sins. He died to make that possible.)

In our second session, we navigated our way to the "Discovery Dens" – homes in which Jesus amazed people as he revealed why he had come.

Stick up "Discovery Dens" coloured visual.

The first home was crammed full as crowds gathered to hear Jesus! It was so packed that when four men arrived carrying their paralyzed friend, they couldn't even get through the door. However, they came up with a plan to dig a hole in the roof and lower him down on his mat. But then the most astonishing thing happened – instead of healing the man, Jesus told him his sins were forgiven.

Have on screen Mark 2:5.
"When Jesus saw their faith, he said to the paralyzed man, 'Son, your sins are forgiven.'"

The friends probably stared through the hole with their mouths wide open. The crowd probably stood still in stunned silence. And the paralyzed man? Well, he probably lay there thinking: "What?! I've not done any-thing to you. My problem's my legs. It's them I need fixing, not my sin!"

But we've discovered this week that *sin* is our biggest problem. Sin means we put ourselves first – we know God is in charge, but we don't treat him as we should. When we do, say or think wrong things – which we all do – we are going against God. We're saying "no" to his ways and his rule.

And the Bible teaches us that sin has serious consequences, because it cuts us off from friendship with God. Sin must be punished. That's why Jesus chose to forgive the man first, rather than healing him.

The religious leaders in the crowd were furious with Jesus, thinking: "He can't do that! He doesn't have the authority!" But he did have the authority. We heard earlier that Jesus is God's Son with God's power – and that includes power to forgive, for all sin is against God.

Jesus knew what the religious leaders were thinking, and knew they couldn't see if he'd actually forgiven the man's sin or not. So Jesus proved he's God by healing the man. The man who was *carried* in, *walked* out, much to the amazement of the onlookers.

So at Breathtaking Bay, our breath was taken away as we heard Jesus' authority in his words and saw it in his actions. Then at the Discovery Dens, we gathered yet more evidence to show us Jesus is God. And we discovered that, because Jesus is God, he has the power to forgive sins too.

Add "Forgiver" under the surprised face at "Discovery Dens".

But how can Jesus forgive us? Well, that's what we discovered at the next place on the island.

Stick up "Mysterious Mountains" coloured visual.

Jesus' words and actions had power. But listen to something really surprising that happened in Mark 15.

Have verses on the screen.

"At noon, darkness came over the whole land until three in the afternoon. And at three in the afternoon Jesus cried out in a loud voice … 'My God, my God, why have you forsaken me?' … With a loud cry, Jesus breathed his last." (Mark 15:33-34, 37)

Jesus' followers must have felt as if they had those glasses with the eyes that pop out. They had heard and seen proof that he is God's Son:

- They saw him heal and forgive people.
- They saw him hero-worshipped.
- They had heard God say: "This is my Son, whom I love".

But then they saw Jesus get beaten, mocked and hung on a cross like a criminal.

And what's more, he had just cried out that God had turned away from him.

Why was Jesus God-forsaken? Why had God turned away from him? Jesus was doing a swap with us, because *we* should be God-forsaken. Our sin means we deserve to be punished. But Jesus, the innocent one, swapped places with us and took our punishment.

> Use the following phone illustration to explain what happened when Jesus died. There's a simplified version, with diagrams, on page 100.

Imagine someone's managed to record all the bad things I've ever done, or you've ever done, on this phone (hold up mobile/cell phone) – such as the lies you've told, the time you let someone down or gossiped behind someone's back. All the times you've lost your temper, had a selfish thought or not treated God as you should. All your sin caught on film. You definitely wouldn't want it on *YouTube*!

Now imagine this hand is me – and the ceiling is where God is. (Put the phone on one hand.) This phone, which shows all my sin, is getting in the way between God and me; my sin separates me from being God's friend.

(Hold out other hand.) Imagine this hand is Jesus. He never did anything wrong so there's nothing separating Jesus and his Father, God. But when Jesus died, he took all my sin (transfer phone from one hand to the other) and the full weight of God's anger at sin was poured out on his own Son, instead of on me.

That's why Jesus cried out in anguish. He was cut off from God's friendship and goodness. Like a headmaster doing our detention, or a judge going to prison on behalf of a prisoner, Jesus took our punishment. He paid the price so our sin could be dealt with, so we can be forgiven friends of God.

Look at my other hand. There's no barrier now. There's nothing separating me from God, because Jesus has taken my sin. That's what happened when he died.

> Add "Died" under the cross on "Mysterious Mountains".

The early explorers often acted out of self-interest as they looked for precious spices, silks and jewels. Jesus acted out of love, despite the fact we rebel against him. He gave his life and sacrificed everything as he travelled to earth, to trade his perfection for our sin; to offer us treasure that far outweighs anything else – life with Jesus, in his kingdom for ever.

But we hadn't finished exploring the island yet. There was more to come…

TALK 3: WHAT DOES IT MEAN TO FOLLOW JESUS?

(Jesus rose to show our sins can be forgiven. We need to choose if we will follow him.)

When we left the Mysterious Mountains, we started to explore Mark 16.

> Stick up the coloured visual for "Crown Cave".

We've seen that Jesus died to forgive sins. But death wasn't the end for Jesus. After he was killed, he was laid in a tomb with a large stone wedged in front. But three days later, people made the best discovery ever – the stone had been moved, the tomb was empty and Jesus had risen.

It was incredible! Jesus had beaten death and was alive, just as he had promised. And because the price he paid for our sin has been accepted by God, we no longer need to be separated from God. We can have new life through Jesus instead – for ever!

Add "Risen" next to the magnifying glass on "Crown Cave".

So, is that the end of the story? After our mind-boggling, binocular-focusing discovery that Jesus died in our place and rose again, surely that's our adventure with him over.

But it isn't. There was one more part of the island to visit as we explored Mark 8.

Stick up the coloured visual for "Rocky Road".

Jesus stayed with his friends for forty days and then returned to heaven. But the Bible promises that one day he will return as King of everything, and the whole world will be under his rule. And we can trust that promise because:

- **Jesus said he would be killed (in Mark 8:31), and he was.**

- **Jesus said he would rise again (in Mark 8:31), and he did.**

- **So, when Jesus said he will come back again (in Mark 8:38) – we can trust that he will! And we should be ready. But how?**

Mark 1:15 says we can be ready by repenting and believing the good news of Jesus.

Display Mark 1 v 15 on the screen: "The time has come," Jesus said. "The kingdom of God has come near. Repent and believe the good news!"

Repenting **means admitting we have done wrong; that we've disobeyed and ignored God. It means we're sorry and now want to live God's way, with him in charge.**

Believing **means we trust that Jesus is God's Son and died in our place. He has done everything we need for us to be forgiven and live as his friends for ever in his perfect kingdom.**

I wonder, will you repent and believe? Will you accept his gift of rescue? Will you follow Jesus?

Add "Follow?" by the gift on the "Rocky Road" visual.

We finished our explorations with this verse from Mark 8:

"Then he called the crowd to him along with his disciples and said: 'Whoever wants to be my disciple must deny themselves and take up their cross and follow me.'" (Mark 8:34)

Being a follower of Jesus is not always easy as it means living to please Jesus and not ourselves, making him the most important. It means we may suffer or be teased for following God. But it also means we know our sins are forgiven, we know God is with us helping us, and we know the secure promise of heaven.

David Livingstone explored much of Southern Africa and discovered the spectacular waterfall of "Victoria Falls". He was also a follower of Jesus. Following the death of his wife and his own ill-health, he said this:

"Anxiety, sickness, suffering, or danger … may make us pause, and cause the spirit to waver, and the soul to sink; but let this only be for a moment. All these are nothing when compared with the glory which shall be revealed in and for us."

David Livingstone knew it was hard to be a follower of Jesus, but he believed it to be worthwhile. Do you?

- **Jesus, God's Son, lived among us.**

- **Jesus died – so our sin can be dealt with and we can be forgiven.**

- **Jesus is alive and can give us life that lasts for ever.**

- **And Jesus will come back again! So we should be ready!**

Maybe you would like to explore things a little further. Why not chat to some of the leaders or take a Mark's Gospel as you leave, and think about things a little more? Maybe you would like to start exploring these things by signing up to our *Christianity Explored* course, which is starting… (give date and plug the course)**.**

Family treasure hunt

Main aims

- To build on relationships and give a brief teaching summary.

- To encourage parents to think about attending a *Christianity Explored* course.

This family treasure hunt is ideal at the end of *Epic Explorers* on a mid-week evening or at a weekend.

You will need:

- Pens
- Clue sheets
- A wall quiz (see page 145)
- Playdough
- Refreshments
- Prizes
- Summary talk for family events (page 142)

Time	Activity		Leader
	Tick when materials are ready for each section	✔	
Before event	Preparation, eg: decorate the room, get games and refreshments ready, etc.		
45 minutes before	Team meeting for prayer and final instructions.		
10 minutes before	Doors open – give families instructions and introduce them to a team member. Let them begin as soon as they are ready.		
60 minutes	Teams complete the treasure hunt. *Note: If is raining, then run the signature bingo quiz as a mixer to start with. You may need to choose some games from pages 145-146 as well.*		
15 minutes	Refreshments Playdough challenge and wall quiz (see page 145)		
10 minutes	Summary talk for family events (see page 142)		
5 minutes	Prizes and announcements		

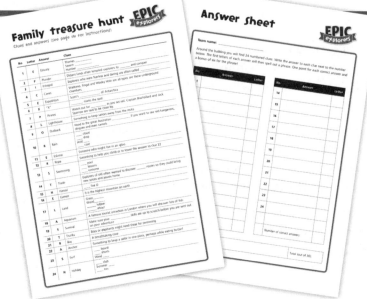

Family treasure hunt (outside)

You will need:

- Maps of the locality, with clue numbers marked on
- Clue sheets, with space for answers
- Pens or pencils
- Volunteers in costume (optional)

1. Match up each family with a team member if possible. This allows for relationship-building as they walk around solving the clues.

2. Give them their map, clue sheet and pen/pencil, and let them know when they need to return by.

3. Rather than following a set route, families can choose their own. Therefore, if they have young children, they may just complete the clues in the immediate area – whereas those of a competitive nature can try to solve them all. This also stops groups bunching up around the route.

4. If you have volunteers in costume scattered around area, the teams also have to collect their signatures. You could add in a question for the families to ask them, eg: "Dr Livingstone, I presume?"

5. Make sure the clues aren't too difficult. Rhyming couplets help create riddles. You could even try to fit them into an explorers theme. Here are some examples, although you will need to adapt them for your own context.

Family treasure hunt (inside)

You will need:

- A5 (half US letter) clues scattered around the building (on an exploration theme)
- Answer sheets (see page 140 for examples – the full sheets can be downloaded from www.ceministries.org/epic)
- Pens or pencils

1. Match up each family with a team member if possible. This allows for relationship-building as they walk around solving the clues.

2. Give them their answer sheet and explain that "x" amount of numbered clues are hidden around the building. When they find a clue, they have to solve it and then write the answer next to the matching number on their sheet.

3. The first letters of each answer will then spell out a phrase. They will get one point for each correct answer and a bonus of six for the phrase.

4. Base your clues on an exploration theme but make sure they aren't too difficult. There are some examples on page 140 (download from www.ceministries.org/epic to be able to read the questions!) – although you will need to adapt them for your own context.

Example clues

It's not Mysterious Mountains
Or even Crown Cave
But here's a great place to get a snack,
If it's food you now crave.

You could use this railway
And discover the sea.
You'll see grey panels on the bridge.
How many can you see?

With clothes of green,
And bark of a dog,
Find out how old I am,
PS: I sleep like a log.

If we were going to the Bay,
We'd need to catch a bus.
What number would you need to catch
So you could come with us?

SUMMARY TALK FOR FAMILY EVENT

Main aim:
- To meet the perfect pioneer, consider the rescue and discover the good news for yourself

You will need:
- A handout for people or a PowerPoint that looks like an Explorer's diary (see page 157. Each point to have a picture of the Bible passage on it with the Bible reference.
- Props for the opening game: hat, sleeping bag, water bottle, compass, binoculars, map and backpack.

This talk outline can also be downloaded from www.ceministries.org/epic

Here are some clues to a person's job – can you guess what is it?

Hold up a backpack and pull the items out, in this order:
- Hat
- Sleeping bag
- Water bottle
- Compass
- Binoculars
- Map

That's right – an explorer. Now, whether you think of the cartoon character, Dora the Explorer; or Christopher Columbus, the European explorer credited with discovering America; or Neil Armstrong, who went to the moon – when you think of explorers, all of them are people who have wanted to find out more and so have set off on adventures, seen amazing sights and discovered new things.

That's exactly what we've been doing too in *Epic Explorers*. We've set off on an adventure, have seen amazing sights and discovered new things, as we've looked not beyond the next mountain or river, but rather, at the life of Jesus. And so, I'd just like to share with you a few of our exciting findings from the Bible book of Mark.

1) Meet the Perfect Pioneer

Show first diary entry.

In 1915 Ernest Shackleton's ship had been trapped in floating ice and sunk; he and his crew had travelled by ice and lifeboats for two months; but Shackleton, the great explorer, was not about to give up. He was determined to rescue his men, and so for 16 days he sailed through stormy seas and trekked over mountains to find help. Shackleton was on a rescue mission for his people. And Jesus was like this. He was on a rescue mission.

How do we know that Jesus can rescue people? Well first, as he began travelling around, he did groundbreaking things – he performed miracles. He wasn't doing it to make money or impress the crowds. Nor was he just trying to show us that he was a nice, caring teacher. Far from it. Jesus was the Perfect Pioneer, performing miracles to show us that he can do things only God can do; that he has power over everything, because he is God's Son.

So, through the amazing sights of Jesus' miracles, we have seen more and more who he is:

- **In Mark 1, we saw how he had authority to teach people. We saw too that he had power over illness and over evil.**

- **If we had read further, we would see in Mark 4 that Jesus also has power over nature. He didn't just *calm* a storm, he stopped it *immediately* with his words.**

- **In Mark 5, Jesus shows he's our loving life-giver; he has power over death. He didn't just *heal* people; he also brought some *back to life*.**

- **In Mark 6, we would discover he's the great and generous provider. He didn't just *feed* the 5000; he had bread and fish *left over*.**

- **And back in Mark 2, we saw that Jesus, God's Son, had power and authority over sin. He didn't just heal the man's *legs*; he dealt with the far bigger problem of the man's *sin* by forgiving him.**

Shackleton longed to rescue his men from Elephant Island – Jesus longs to rescue us from the punishment we deserve. He longs to forgive us. All of us need this rescue because all of us fail to treat God as we should, whether it's the way we are selfish in our decisions, or disobedient in our actions, or we simply ignore him. We deserve to be punished for our sin, and that's why we need rescuing by the Perfect Pioneer: the one who is God.

2) Consider the rescue

Show second diary entry.

Shackleton succeeded in reaching a whaler's station, and with the help of a team of men and a Navy tug boat, he rescued his 22 men. They were saved, having spent four and a half months on Elephant Island. He returned to Britain a national hero. But he became a heavy drinker, and died five years later while on another Antarctic expedition.

While Shackleton's rescue was undoubtedly heroic, it was also limited – he saved 22 lives. Jesus' rescue was so much greater than this. Jesus came to provide a way of rescue for everyone. He came to forgive sins.

And yet his rescue plan seemed to go so wrong. Jesus – the perfect, powerful Son of God – was arrested and sentenced to death. He was nailed to a cross and left to die. And there wasn't a Hollywood hero who took him down from the cross. Jesus died.

But the amazing thing is that this was all part of the rescue plan. He died in our place, taking God's punishment for all the wrong we ever say, think and do; for the times we lie and we lose our temper with our brother or sister. For the times we gossip or we cheat our employers. For the times we don't treat God as we should.

We read in Mark 15 that Jesus chose to take what we deserve – separation from God's friendship and goodness – so he could offer his perfection to us and make a way possible for us to be forgiven. Jesus didn't just come to show us he was the Son of God, but also how we can *know* God.

We discovered in Mark 16 that Jesus' death was not the end – that just as he had promised, he came alive three days later. Many saw him, spoke with him and ate with him. He showed that his words can be trusted, that his power conquers all, and that there is now a way for us to be friends with God for ever. That's why no one else is better and why his rescue is the greatest – it's everlasting and offered to everyone.

3) Discover the good news for yourself

Show third diary entry.

Shackleton's Antarctic expeditions were driven by his desire to discover. On his final trip, he had heard about some lost islands and so went to find them.

As we've been exploring the life of Jesus in the book of Mark, we've heard about the good news of "Jesus the Messiah, the Son of God" (Mark 1:1). We've not only seen Jesus revealing that he's the Son of God, and all that he offered, but we've also discovered how people responded to him. Some chose to ignore him; others felt threatened; but still others believed and were changed. They thanked him and followed him, even though it wouldn't always be easy.

I wonder how you respond to Jesus.

- Think about who he is – we've discovered he is none other than God Almighty. He's powerful and full of authority.

- Think about what he's like – he loves you enough to rescue you, by dying for you. So why wouldn't you want to follow him?

- And think about why following him is such a good thing – because he wants to rescue you.

Are you driven by a desire to discover? Would you like to find out more? Why not chat to some of the leaders tonight or take a Mark's Gospel as you leave and think about things a little more? Maybe you would like to start exploring things by signing up to our *Christianity Explored* course, which is starting... (give date and plug the course).

Family fun night

Main aims

■ To celebrate *Epic Explorers* and to give a brief teaching summary.

■ To encourage parents to think about attending a *Christianity Explored* course.

This family fun night is ideal at the end of *Epic Explorers* on a mid-week evening or at a weekend.

You will need:

- Pens and score sheets
- Team posters (famous explorers)
- Materials for your choice of games
- Joker cards
- Refreshments
- Prizes
- Summary talk (page 142)
- Quiz questions and scoreboard

Time	Activity		Leader
	Tick when materials are ready for each section	✔	
Before event	Preparation, eg: decorate, get games and refreshments ready, etc.		
45 min before	Team meeting for prayer and final instructions		
5 min before (for 15 min)	Doors open Playdough challenge and wall quiz (see page 145)		
3 min	Give a brief introduction; then split entire group into 4 or 6 equal teams. All the teams to compete at the same time, all playing the same game together, against the other teams. Each team has a Joker card, which they can opt to play on one round and double the points they earn on that particular game – but they must declare the Joker beforehand.		
7 min	All teams play Bring me (page 145)		
7 min	All teams build a ship (page 145)		
5 min	Representatives from each team play Jousting (page 145)		
6 min	All teams complete the screen test (page 146)		
5 min	Food tasting (page 146)		
7 min	All teams play Pictionary (page 146)		
5 min	Representatives from each team go on a "plank expedition" (p 146)		
7 min	All teams join in the Battle (page 146)		
15 min	Refreshments and quiz (use one from the week)		
10 min	Summary talk for family events (see page 142)		
5 min	Prizes and announcements		

Note: Try to choose a variety of games that will include everyone and need a range of skills. The games above are suggestions. You may want to replace some or all with other games from pages 49-52.

Ideas menu

Playdough challenge

You will need:

- Lots of playdough (bought or make your own)

1. As families arrive, ask them to create a previously undiscovered animal that they have stumbled across on their recent expedition to distant lands.

2. Announce the winner of the most creative design.

Wall quiz

You will need:

- Pictures to stick on the wall
- Blu-tack reuseable adhesive
- Answer sheets
- Pens

1. Beforehand, crop some images of explorer items, eg: compass, backpack, binoculars. Print them off and stick them on the wall of the area you are meeting in.

2. As families arrive, explain that they have to go around and look at the different pictures, trying to discover what the mystery items are.

3. Mark the answers.

Bring me

You will need:

- A list of items to be found eg:
- Something soft to rest your head on
- Sheep's wool
- Something gold
- Money to pay your ship's fare
- Something to tell you the time
- Something sweet-smelling like spices
- A book for your findings to be recorded in
- Something you can climb
- A piece of wood to build a raft
- A picture of royalty

- Something to cover a head with

Each team is to designate a runner. Call out an item from the list for the team to find. Their runner must bring the item to you – the first one to do so scores a point. Continue until the list is finished. Award points.

Build a ship

You will need:

- Boxes
- Brown tape
- Scrap paper
- Scissors
- Bin bags

Give each team a selection of junk. They have five minutes to create a ship to sail the Seven Seas in! Award points for team work and creativity.

Jousting

You will need:

- 4 or 6 light wooden (unbreakable) trays / foil platters
- 4 or 6 rolled-up newspapers (held with tape) of equal size (the lances)

1. Ask each team to send up a representative adult. They will each be given a tray and a newspaper lance.

2. They have to return to their teams and stand on one leg, balancing the tray on one hand, and holding the "lance" in the other.

3. When you shout go, they must hop into the middle and try to knock the other person's tray out of their hand using the newspaper lance. If they drop their tray or hold onto it, then they are out. Points awarded to the last one in.

4. Repeat with a child representative from each team.

Screen test

You will need:
- A DVD
- A way of projecting the film clip
- Paper
- Pens

1. Show the teams a three-minute clip from "Dora the Explorer" or something else on an exploration theme.

2. Ask 15 questions based upon what they have seen and heard.

3. Mark the answers and award points accordingly.

Food tasting

You will need:
- Baby food
- Paper plates
- Plastic spoons
- Paper and pens

1. Beforehand, buy a number of jars of baby food. Put a teaspoonful of each type onto 4 or 6 paper plates.

2. Ask the teams to send up a representative to come and taste the delights from distant lands.

3. Award points to those who correctly identify the food.

Pictionary

You will need:
- List of 15 explorer items, eg: compass, map, hat
- Paper
- Pens

1. Ask for one person from each team to come to you and collect a word which they need to draw for the rest of their team.

2. When their team has guessed correctly, they send up another "draw-er". They collect the next word and draw it for the team.

3. Continue until the list is completed. Award points accordingly.

Plank expedition

You will need:
- Planks of wood
- Five representatives from each team.

1. Ask for five representatives to come up from each team. Each group of five has to stand in a line, one behind another.

2. Give each team two planks of wood.

3. They have to try and transport themselves using the wood, from one side of the room to the other, without their feet touching the ground.

4. Award points for the team of five who get there first.

Battle

You will need:
- Chairs or marker cones
- Scrunched-up scrap paper

1. Divide room into 4 or 6 areas.

2. Give each team 30 scrunched-up balls of scrap paper.

3. Teams to throw the balls at other teams while trying to keep them out of their own zone. The team that has the least each time the whistle blows gains points.

Appendices

EPIC EXPLORERS DRAMA
Five children explore Adventure Island

HOW THE DRAMA WORKS

The drama is designed to illustrate the children's experience of *Epic Explorers*. It is made up of five acts* with five characters.** Each act is made up of three parts:

Rhymes (Core)
All six rhymes are to be recited at the beginning of each act (the Narration rhyme plus the five Character rhymes). This is to reinforce the whole story, which is particularly important for children who may not be able to attend all the *Epic Explorers* sessions. The rhymes will act as "opening credits".

Scene 1 (Optional)
This assumes that you have five actors and is primarily to give the children opportunity to get to know the characters better.

Scene 2 (Core)
This is more plot driven and can be performed by two actors if the lines for Crop and Berry are combined.

As the drama progresses, the number of characters decreases as, one by one, they choose to remain where they are rather than continue their journey. There are loose connections with the various seeds and soils in the parable of the sower from Mark chapter 4. During the course of the drama, the characters discover four clues to direct their journey. The clues take the form of jigsaw pieces which, when assembled, create a "FOLLOW ME" sign.

Crop's songs can be sung live or played using a recording to which he will mime the words.

* More than one act could be performed at any one time. Suggested breakdown for a four-day club is to combine acts 3 and 4.

** If you only have two actors, one would play Berry and Crop combined, and the other would play Beak, Rosie and Sonny; changing costumes/props as necessary.

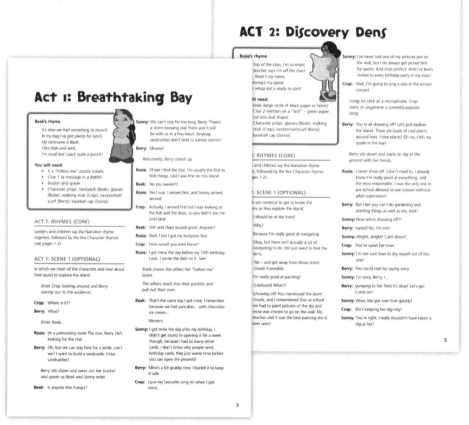

RHYMES

Narration Rhyme

*Five children arrived so excited
on the island where they'd been invited.
They were told "Follow me"
and now we will see
if anyone went home delighted.*

CHARACTERS

Robert **"Beak"** Beak, 9-year-old boy
Likes: Food
Known for: Being hungry!
Costume/prop: Backpack

*It's time we had something to munch.
In my bag I've got plenty for lunch.
My nickname is Beak,
I like hide and seek,
I'm small but I pack quite a punch!*

Rosie **"Rosie"** Morgan,
10-year-old girl
Likes: Winning
Known for: Being good at things
Costume/prop: Glasses

*I'm top of the class, I'm so smart,
My teacher says I'm off the chart.
Yes, Rosie's my name,
Exploring's my game.
This whizz-kid is ready to start!*

Alex **"Crop"** Cropper, 9-year-old boy
Likes: Music
Known for: Singing
Costume/prop: A tall walking stick

*Hey people, my nickname is Crop!
My music is ready to drop.
If you're hiking too slow,
I'll sing as we go.
We'll make it right up to the top!*

Polly **"Berry"** Berry, 8-year-old girl
Likes: Gardening
Known for: Being muddy!
Costume/prop: Neckerchief/scarf

*I'm Berry – I like things that grow.
You'll find me in mud head to toe!
I wear my green boots
When digging up roots.
I can't wait to see where we will go!*

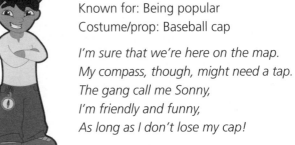
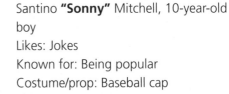

Santino **"Sonny"** Mitchell, 10-year-old
boy
Likes: Jokes
Known for: Being popular
Costume/prop: Baseball cap

*I'm sure that we're here on the map.
My compass, though, might need a tap.
The gang call me Sonny,
I'm friendly and funny,
As long as I don't lose my cap!*

The full drama is available for free download from www.ceministries.org/epic

"EPIC EXPLORERS"

Lively, with energy

Nick Rhydderch, Tamar Pollard

Em D C   C D Em D C   D B⁷/D♯

Chorus

5 Em   C   D   Em

"Ep - ic Ex - plo — rers" — we're stan - ding on the shore.___

9 Em   C   Am⁷   C/D D

You've heard the sto - ries! Now, come and find out more! See the

13 G B⁷/D♯   Em Bm⁷   C Am⁷   D B⁷/D♯

One who gave him - self to save us - Frees us from our___ sin

Last time to CODA

17 Em   C   D   Em

"Ep - ic Ex - plo - rers" let's get ad- ven - tur - ing!

150

2

Verse ("*Half speed*" *feel*)

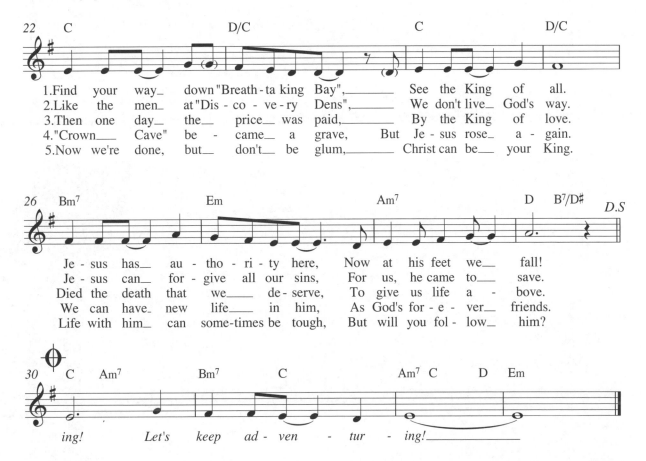

C	D/C	C	D/C

1.Find your way_ down "Breath-ta king Bay",_____ See the King of all.
2.Like the men_ at "Dis - co - ve - ry Dens",_____ We don't live_ God's way.
3.Then one day_ the_ price_ was paid,_____ By the King of love.
4."Crown___ Cave" be - came_ a grave, But Je - sus rose_ a - gain.
5.Now we're done, but_ don't_ be glum,_____ Christ can be_ your King.

Bm⁷	Em	Am⁷	D B⁷/D♯ *D.S*

Je - sus has_ au - tho - ri - ty here, Now at his feet we_ fall!
Je - sus can_ for - give all our sins, For us, he came to_ save.
Died the death that we_____ de - serve, To give us life a - bove.
We can have_ new life_____ in him, As God's for - e - ver_ friends.
Life with him_ can some-times be tough, But will you fol - low_ him?

C Am⁷	Bm⁷	C	Am⁷ C D Em

ing! Let's keep ad - ven - tur - ing!_____

Actions for the chorus:

"Epic Explorers" (arms in an "x" in front of chest)

– we're standing (point down at the ground)

on the shore. (hands palm down, move horizontally outwards)

You've heard the stories! (point at others in front),

Now, come and find out more! (beckon in)!

See the One who gave himself to save us – (arms out in a cross shape)

Frees us from our sin. (wrists crossed, in front of stomach – then pull them apart, as if breaking free)

"Epic Explorers" (arms in an "x" in front of chest)

– let's get adventuring! (take a few steps to one side)

Sheet music, including full piano score, is available for free download from www.ceministries.org/epic

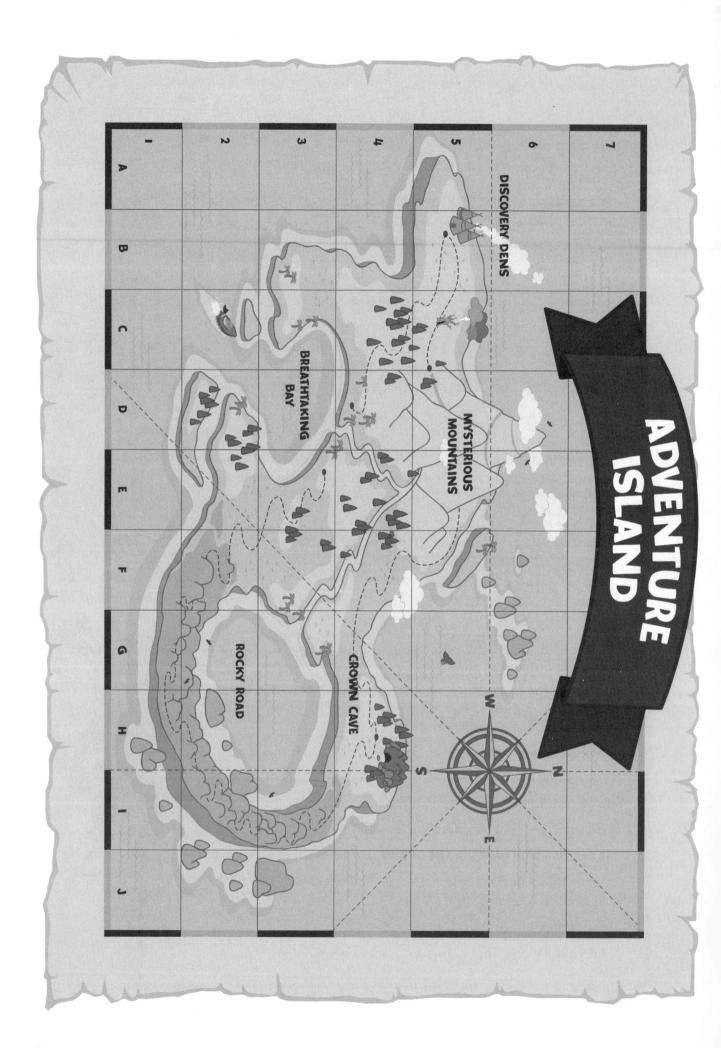

152

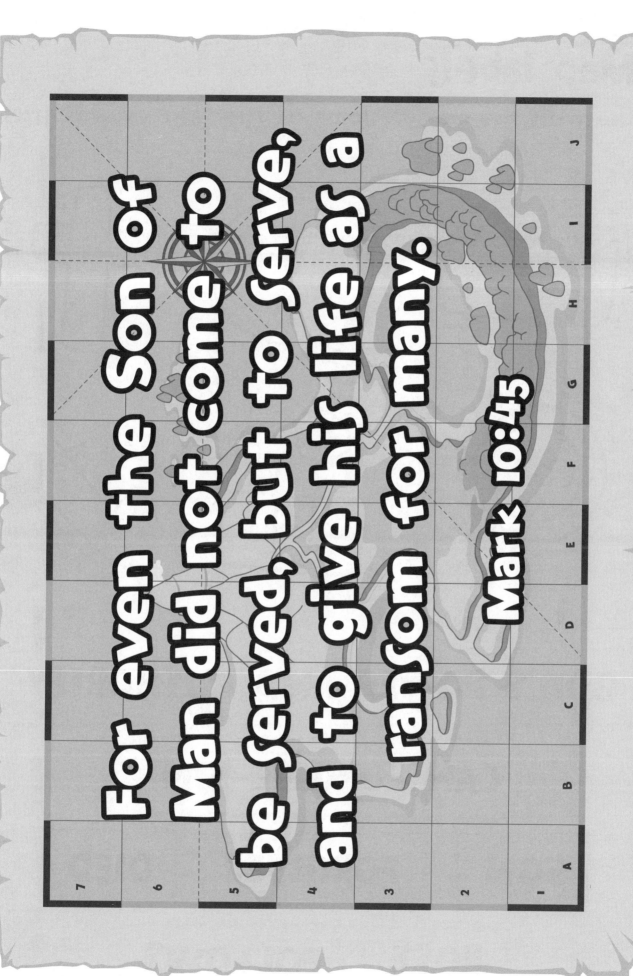

For even the Son of Man did not come to be served, but to serve, and to give his life as a ransom for many.

Mark 10:45

Map labels

Use with the map for some of the talks and activities

GOD'S POWER AND AUTHORITY

CAN FORGIVE SIN

SON FORGIVER DIED

ROSE FOLLOW?

Foget about ourselves, pick up our cross, and follow Jesus

MARK 1

MARK 2

MARK 15

MARK 16

MARK 8

Explorer Notebook

Explorer Notebook visual aid

In each of the five main sessions, Talk Idea 2 uses an "Explorer Notebook" as one of the visual aids. Make the notebook from a large spiral book, or by inserting pages into a ring file or plastic wallets. The pages should be laid out as below so that the next stage is revealed each time you turn a page.

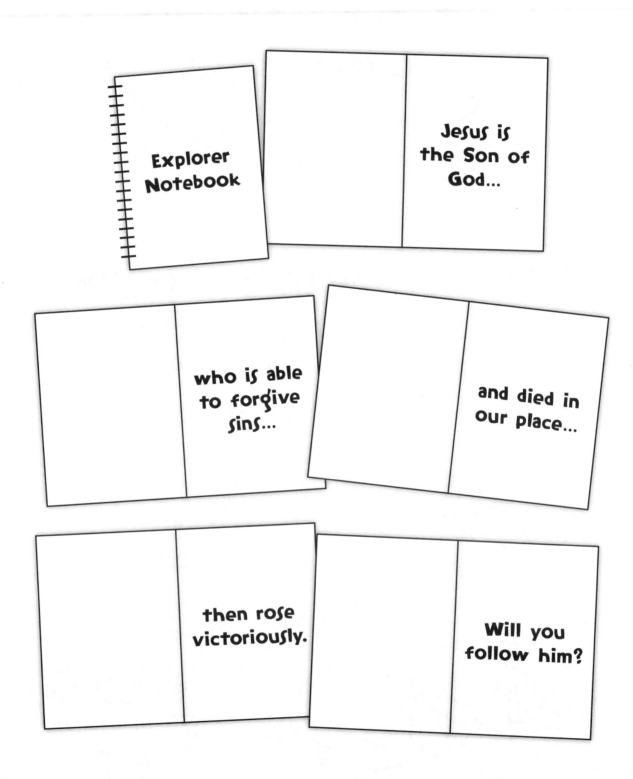

Memory verse

FOR EVEN THE SON OF MAN

DID NOT COME TO BE SERVED BUT TO SERVE

AND TO GIVE HIS LIFE AS A RANSOM FOR MANY

MARK 10:45

Explorer's Diary visuals

Explorer's Diary visual aids

The summary talk for the family events (page 142) uses a visual of an Explorer's Diary to sum up the teaching from Mark's Gospel. This can be displayed on PowerPoint, or printed as a handout. Available to download from:

www.ceministries.org/epic

Finger puppets

Acknowledgements...

Epic Explorers was written by Nate Morgan Locke and Tamar Pollard, and edited by Barry Cooper and Alison Mitchell.

Special thanks to our panel of children's leaders, and the team at *Christianity Explored*, who have trialled *Epic Explorers* and given hugely helpful feedback:

Sarah Bradley, Helen Buckley, Ali Campbell Smith, Nicole Carter, Ed Drew, Stuart Chaplin, Olly Elliott, Dean and Mary Faulkner, Mike Jones, Julie Noonan, Heather Payne, Nick Rhydderch, Karen Sanders, Ben Shaw, Jenny Singh, David Sprouse, Tim Thornborough, Mark Tomlinson and Anne Woodcock.

Design by André Parker and ninefootone creative. Illustration by André Parker.

Christianity Explored Ministries (CEM) aims to provide Christian churches and organisations worldwide with resources which explain the Christian faith clearly and relevantly from the Bible. CEM receives royalties from the sale of these resources, but is reliant on donations for the majority of its income. CEM is registered for charitable purposes in both the United Kingdom and the USA.

www.ceministries.org

Christianity EXPLORED

THE GOSPEL FOR EVERYONE

Every version of *Christianity Explored* uses Mark's Gospel to explore who Jesus is, why he came and what it means to follow him. But each version is specially tailored to make the gospel as clear as possible to the target audience.

For more information, including *Christianity Explored* for adults, visit **www.ceministries.org**

Epic Explorers: Christianity Explored for 4-11 year olds

Epic Explorers Leader's Guide

Everything you need to run *Epic Explorers*, including games, activities, craft templates and talk outlines.

Epic Explorers Logbook and Scratch Pad

Ideal to use with children during *Epic Explorers*. The *Logbook* is designed for 8-11s and the *Scratch Pad* with 4-7s.

CY: Christianity Explored for 11-14 year olds

CY Leader's Guide

All the help you need to run the course, including games, activities and talk outlines.

CY Handbook

For all group members; includes session outlines, cartoons and much more...

Soul: Christianity Explored for 15 years old+

Soul DVD

Beautifully produced with on-screen Bible text and animated illustrations. Includes Spanish subtitles.

Soul Leader's Guide

Contains session outlines and advice on running the Soul course.

Soul Handbook

This Handbook is designed for group members on the Soul course.

Mark's Gospel

Perfect to give group members to use alongside their Handbooks.

Supporting downloads available from:

www.ceministries.org/epic

- **Talk outlines** – Copies of the talks for the 5 main sessions and for the family events are available both as pdfs and in Word format, so that you can personalize each talk with your own illustrations etc.

- **Visual aids** – A number of visual aids can be downloaded to show during the talks.

- **Notes for discussion groups** – Comprehensive leader's notes to use alongside the *Epic Scratch Pad* (4-7s) and *Epic Logbook* (8-11s).

- **Resources for activities** – Includes craft templates, treasure-hunt clues, score sheets, etc.

- **Extra ideas** – There are so many exciting ideas to use with *Epic Explorers* that we can't fit them all in the book! See online for further crafts, games, quizzes, introductory activities and ideas for decorating the venue.

- **Drama and song** – The full script for the five-part drama, and sheet music for the theme song, are both available online, along with a recording of the song.

- **Team training material** – Includes programme outlines, timetables, training sessions, team devotions, and a comprehensive list of answers to common questions from Mark's Gospel.

- **Forms** – These include permission forms for before the event, and feedback forms to use afterwards. Sample forms are available on the website in a variety of designs and sizes.

- **Logos for your own publicity** – If you are going to create your own printed invitations to the course, you can download copies of the *Epic Explorers* logo, which is available in a number of formats.